Virginia Born Presidents

CENTRAL HALL OF THE STATE CAPITOL

Showing the statue of George Washington by Houdon, the bust of John Tyler by Keck, and the bust of Zachary Taylor by Sievers.

Virginia Born Presidents

ADDRESSES DELIVERED ON THE OCCASIONS
OF UNVEILING THE BUSTS OF VIRGINIA
BORN PRESIDENTS AT OLD HALL OF
THE HOUSE OF DELEGATES
RICHMOND, VIRGINIA

*Compiled under the Auspices of and
With an Introduction by*

THE HONORABLE JNO. GARLAND POLLARD

Essay Index Reprint Series

BOOKS FOR LIBRARIES PRESS
FREEPORT, NEW YORK

First Published 1932
Reprinted 1971

INTERNATIONAL STANDARD BOOK NUMBER:
0-8369-2300-6

LIBRARY OF CONGRESS CATALOG CARD NUMBER:
79-156728

PRINTED IN THE UNITED STATES OF AMERICA

CONTENTS

ILLUSTRATIONS

THE HONORABLE JNO. GARLAND POLLARD

Governor of Virginia

PREFACE

BY

THE HONORABLE JNO. GARLAND POLLARD

Governor of Virginia

The General Assembly of Virginia by an Act, approved March 8, 1930, provided that, " under the direction of the Governor and the Art Commission, organizations, societies, or persons may be permitted to place busts of white marble, of uniform size in the several niches of the rotunda of the Capitol, the locations of which shall be, beginning with the niche to the west of the door leading to the entrance to the south portico of the Capitol, the bust of Thomas Jefferson and, in regular order, succeeding and continuing to the right, the bust of James Madison, James Monroe, William Henry Harrison, John Tyler, Zachary Taylor and Woodrow Wilson."

This Act was written by Colonel John W. Williams, veteran Clerk of the House of Delegates and Keeper of the Rolls of Virginia, and was favorably reported to the General Assembly by a committee composed of Lieutenant Governor James H. Price, Henry T. Wickham, and Hunter Miller, on the part of the Senate; and Speaker J. Sinclair Brown, R. L. Brewer, Jr., and Frank Moore, on the part of the House of Delegates.

In the summer of 1930 on the occasion of a visit to Ashlawn, one of the former homes of James Monroe, I mentioned the foregoing Act to a party there gathered consisting of Mr. and Mrs. Jay W. Johns, Rev. N. Addison Baker, Theodore Fred Kuper, Mrs. Thomas W. Murrell and Mrs. Virginia Taylor. I informed them of my intention during my term of office to transform the rotunda into the Hall of the Presidents as contemplated by the Act. My statement was enthusiastically received, and, to my delight, Mr. Baker, Mr. Johns and Mr. Kuper each offered to procure the donation of a bust.

With this encouraging beginning I at once let the plan be known to persons whom I thought might be interested. The response was immediate and hearty.

The bust of Thomas Jefferson was donated by French friends and admirers, Jean Tillier, Chairman, at the solicitation of Mr. Kuper, and is the work of Attilio Piccirilli after the original by Jean Antoine Houdon in the New York Historical Society; those of James Madison and Zachary Taylor were donated by their kinsman, Jaquelin P. Taylor, and F. William Sievers is the sculptor; the bust of James Monroe was donated by Mr. Jay W. Johns and is the work of Attilio Piccirilli; the bust of William Henry Harrison was the gift of William Steele Gray III, David Dunlop Gray, and John Stuart Gray, the children of Mr. and Mrs. William S. Gray; the bust of John Tyler was given upon the solicitation of the Reverend N. Addison Baker by Jessie Ball DuPont, wife of Alfred I. DuPont, and Charles Keck is the sculptor. The bust of Woodrow Wilson is the work of Harriet Frishmuth and was donated by Mr. and Mrs. Louis Pennington.

The sculptors for the busts were selected by the donors with the approval of the Virginia Art Commission composed of Philip N. Stern, Chairman, Dr. Edmund S. Campbell, secretary, Gari Melchers, Wickham C. Taylor, and the Governor.

As the time approached for the unveiling of these works of art, my attention was called to the fact that the famous Houdon statue of George Washington, which occupies the center of the rotunda, had been erected in 1796 without ceremony. It was thought fitting, especially in view of the approaching Washington Bicentennial Celebrations, to begin the ceremonies by an address on George Washington, the first of the Virginia born Presidents.

I accordingly invited Albert Bushnell Hart, A.B., Ph.D., Litt.D., LL.D., of Massachusetts to deliver the address. The Washington ceremonies were held on May 14th, 1931, on the one hundred thirty-fifth anniversary of the creation of the statue, when Dr. Hart appeared dressed in Colonial costume and made an address *nunc pro tunc*, representing himself as a Massachusetts gentleman who had come to Virginia in 1796 to pay tribute to the Father of Our Country.

The ceremonies in honor of succeeding Presidents and the unveiling of their busts took place in quick succession according to the programs hereinafter set forth. Each ceremony was nationally broadcast through the courtesy of the National Broadcasting Company. The ceremonies were held in the old Hall of the House of Delegates of the ancient Capitol designed by Thomas Jefferson and first occupied in 1789. In this hall Aaron Burr had been tried for treason in 1807, General Lee had received in 1861 his commission as Commander of the military forces of Virginia, and within its four walls had met the Congress of the Confederate States. At each unveiling matchless orators, before brilliant audiences, recalled deeds of greatness from Washington to Wilson.

An interesting feature of the occasion was the presence, as special guests, of the descendants and relatives of the Presidents, for whom receptions were given at the Executive Mansion following the ceremonies. In the case of the unveiling of the bust of Woodrow Wilson, the occasion was graced by the presence of his widow, former members of his Cabinet, and his physician, Admiral Cary T. Grayson.

As Governor of the Commonwealth I here again record my sincere thanks to the generous donors of these busts, to the orators who so ably and graphically interpreted their subjects, to the National Broadcasting Company for making it possible for us to multiply by many times those who were privileged to enjoy the addresses, to Colonel John W. Williams and Robert Lecky, Jr., for their valuable service in arranging for the ceremonies, and to all others who aided in making these occasions successful.

The addresses which follow are published with the hope that they may stimulate interest in the history of our country, and especially that they may be inspiring to the young men and women in our schools and colleges.

JNO. GARLAND POLLARD
Governor of Virginia

GEORGE WASHINGTON

President of the United States

1789–1797

DR. ALBERT BUSHNELL HART IN COLONIAL COSTUME

FROM THE INTRODUCTION OF THE SPEAKER

by

JOHN STEWART BRYAN

Today Virginia inaugurates a series of commemorative exercises in honor of her sons who have served their day and generation from the exalted seat of President of the United States of America.

It is a natural but happy coincidence that holds this celebration in this Capitol which Jefferson, the architect, with prehensive genius, adapted from the Maison Carrée *of Nímes.*

When this building was erected in 1785, no one, not even the most sanguine and self-satisfied, imagined that within the space of one hundred and thirty-four years Virginia would have given birth to eight of the thirty-one Presidents. Yet there they are: Washington, Jefferson, Madison, Monroe, Harrison, Tyler, Taylor, Wilson. And there, too, are set apart with almost prophetic foresight, the eight spaces for those marble effigies.

One hundred and thirty-five years ago this statue of Washington was here placed, and it would seem perhaps to the querulous that it is unnecessary to recall — when the statue itself has stood here for more than a century and a quarter — the fact that Virginia had officially, with boundless love, admiration, gratitude, and reverence, here set this stone in perpetual memory of her greatest son.

But it would be impossible to carry out Governor Pollard's splendid conception without first paying homage anew to George Washington, who led the way and who, in his life and service, set up a mark of genius in war, of achievement in peace, and of glory in personality that have placed him not only securely above all his fellow-citizens, but among the first rank of those who in

JEAN ANTOINE HOUDON, *The Sculptor*

recorded history have lighted up and led mankind in their several ages.

Today it is with a sense of profound emotion that, as I contemplate the passage of time for more than a generation, I see the healing balm that has flowed from the work of such generous historians as Dr. Albert Bushnell Hart, who has come to deliver this address, dressed in costume of 1796. He is a friend of Virginians, and a friend of Virginia; a profound student of American history, and one who grasped by intuition and confirmed by research the illimitable reaches of fortitude, patriotism, wisdom, and majesty in the character of George Washington.

GEORGE WASHINGTON

ADDRESS

AS OF MAY 14TH, 1796

BY

ALBERT BUSHNELL HART, LL.D.

Your Excellency, Assemblage of Virginia Beauty, Members of the Assembly, Citizens of Virginia, Friends and Admirers of our venerated President George Washington:

We are met to consummate a purpose first formed nearly thirteen years ago, when the United States in Congress Assembled voted unanimously that "an equestrian statue of General Washington be erected at the place where the residence of Congress shall be established." That place has recently been selected, and to it has been given the name of the Republic's Commander-in-Chief and later President, although at this moment he is at the temporary capital at Philadelphia, detained by public duties — else he would be the guest of honor on this occasion.

It is true that the expectation of Congress in its vote of 1783 was that he should be "represented in a Roman dress, holding a truncheon in his right hand, and his head encircled with a laurel wreath." It has not yet been carried out, but you are aware that the Virginia Legislature eleven years ago resolved that "the Executive be requested to take measures for procuring a statue of General Washington, to be of the finest marble and the best workmanship." Members of that Legislature present today will remember how our great fellow citizen, James Madison, on that occasion wrote upon his knee as a member of the Legislature the stirring words which today are incised upon the statue:

THE GENERAL ASSEMBLY OF THE COMMONWEALTH OF VIRGINIA
HAVE CAUSED THIS STATUE TO BE ERECTED
AS A MONUMENT OF AFFECTION AND GRATITUDE TO
GEORGE WASHINGTON
WHO
UNITING TO THE ENDOWMENTS OF THE HERO THE VIRTUES OF THE
PATRIOT AND EXERTING BOTH IN ESTABLISHING THE
LIBERTIES OF HIS COUNTRY HAS RENDERED HIS NAME
DEAR TO HIS FELLOW CITIZENS AND
GIVEN THE WORLD AN IMMORTAL EXAMPLE
OF TRUE GLORY

The home-State of Washington has outrun its fellow States in Congress assembled, although twelve years have elapsed since Virginia's purpose was formed. The State has but preceded the Nation in perpetuating in marble or enduring brass the features of our beloved President and most eminent son of Virginia.

Need I remind gentlemen here, some of whom must have participated in the original vote of 1785, of the service of another great son of Virginia, Thomas Jefferson, throughout his adult life a leader in the public affairs of this Commonwealth, and fortunately for our patriotic purpose, Minister of the United States to France at the time of the vote of the Legislature. Mr. Jefferson, whose seat at Monticello has doubtless received as guests many of the ladies and gentlemen here present, took up this declared purpose of the State with enthusiasm and success. He was aided by Dr. Franklin, long in the public service of the Colonies and the United States, who lived till but a few years ago.

At the request of Governor Harrison, who eleven years ago occupied the gubernatorial throne, Mr. Jefferson entered into negotiations with that renowned statuary, Jean Antoine Houdon, already famous for his work in clay and bronze and marble. He reported that Houdon possessed "the reputation of being the first statuary in the world." The statue standing in the Rotunda is the evidence of his supreme abilities in the artistic field. He declined to make a life-size statue of a man whom he had never seen, even from the portrait which Governor Harrison ordered for that purpose from Charles Wilson Peale, who has made several excellent portraits of our beloved President. Jefferson as you are aware speedily reported that this sculptor, for a payment of one thousand English guineas (something like five thousand Spanish dollars), would prepare statue and pedestal, provided arrangements were made, at the cost of the State of Virginia, for Houdon to come to the United States and mold the lineaments of Virginia's greatest son. We may congratulate ourselves that Houdon with some difficulty withdrew himself from a preceding commission ordained by the Empress of Russia, because he considered the artistic confidence of Virginia "as promising the brightest chapter of his history."

When the diary of President Washington is opened for the inspection of his countrymen, we shall be aware of the exact circumstances of the contact between the great General and the great Statuary. We know that Washington wrote to Houdon, "It will give me pleasure, Sir, to welcome you to this seat of my retirement; and whatever I have, or can procure, that is necessary to your purposes, or convenient and agreeable to your wishes, you must freely command, as inclination to oblige you will be among the last things in which I shall be found deficient, either on your arrival or during your stay."

Perhaps a century hence that section of the President's diary will come to be published in which he has inscribed the names and conversation of some of the distinguished citizens of Virginia here present. Our descendants will then know some of the incidents of Houdon's stay at Mount Vernon from October 2 to October 17, 1785, during which time our fellow citizen James Madison was also a visitor. Happily the artist left behind him, besides the bust which he took with him as the basis of our statue, also another bust incorporating the lineaments of the great man which will one day become one of the choicest treasures of that chaste and ornamental mansion, Mount Vernon. Some wealthy merchant in such a commercial city as New York, mayhap a hundred years hence, will come into possession of that Parisian bust for the advantage of the American people. Fortunately for us, Jefferson has used his influence with Houdon to avoid the pompous costume of the ancient Romans intended by the vote of Congress. Thus comes about that John Marshall, our young jurist, who some day may be inscribed in the register of Virginia's great sons, considers that to a spectator standing on the right hand of the statue and taking a half-heightened front view "it represented the original as perfectly as a living man could be represented in marble."

Monsieur Houdon is still active in his profession, and it is predicted that perhaps a century hence the French Government will set apart a section of a great art museum for the work of that renowned artist. Had the purpose of Congress been carried out, the city of Washington would today possess an equestrian statue of Washington in his continental uniform from the same unrivaled hand as the statue which we dedicate today.

Do we here need to be reminded of the circumstances of the recent completion of the statue? It was so nearly ready eight years ago that the sculptor placed upon it the date of 1788. James Monroe, another of Virginia's famous sons, urged completion of the project upon both Virginia and Houdon. Only four months ago the statue, inclosed in three cases, was placed on board the ship *Planter*, Ayres Stockley, Master, bound for Philadelphia. It reached Philadelphia last month and thence was conveyed unto the order of a Norfolk merchant to "said Governor and Council of Richmond or to his orders and assignments." Thus it has been completely placed in time for this dedication of May 14, 1796. A small amount is claimed by the artist for adherent expenses which will shortly be satisfied. You, gallant gentlemen and lovely ladies, are distinguished by this first opportunity to behold the master work of a renowned sculptor.

We are informed that Houdon five years ago made what we assume to be a replica of this statue for presentation to the Marquis de LaFayette. In the distant future, aye far off in the twentieth century, it may be the privilege of Virginia to present a copy, perhaps in bronze, to the government of a sister republic. We are all aware that in the last few months has come forward in the distressed affairs of France a notable young general Bonaparte, married to the widow of the brave Frenchman, Beauharnais, who was one of the spirited young officers to participate with us fifteen years ago in the final battles of the Revolution.

Such, Your Excellency, is the brief account of the manner in which Virginia has now become the possessor of the magnificent work of art which we are to dedicate today. At the outset my mind is imbued with trepidation at the responsibility incurred by a citizen of Massachusetts who, by undue confidence upon the part of the Governor, is commissioned to this important service. How shall a plain New Englander, a teacher of young men, a writer of books, and editor of other men's literary work, speak where the princes of American oratory have opened the minds and aroused the souls of Virginia's proudest and fairest? Perhaps, Sir, I am here today because my State of Massachusetts is the elder of the Northern group of colonies, as Virginia is the elder of the Southern group. You Virginians are proud of John Smith, doughty warrior, bold explorer, your predecessor, Sir, in the governance of the Commonwealth of Virginia, but John Smith also knew New England and named many of the places on our coast. From the time that there were two recognized colonies of Virginia and Massachusetts there has been active trade between the northern and the southern settlements. Some Virginia families settled in New England. Who knows but the descendant of a Virginia Jefferson may yet be allied in marriage with a Massachusetts Coolidge? Within the two Commonwealths sprang up the first two American colleges, Harvard and William and Mary. Virginians and Massachusetts men in recent years have sat together in Carpenters Hall and the Federal Hall. It was John Adams, a Massachusetts member of the Second Continental Congress, Sir, at present Vice President of the United States, who proposed George Washington of Virginia to be Commander-in-Chief of the Continental Armies.

We of Massachusetts received him with honor and military obedience. His name stands on the brief roll of men honored by the President and Fellows of Harvard College with the degree of LL.D., an institution of which I have the honor to be an humble A.B. For nearly a year George Washington exercised his vast intellect on the siege of Boston; and twenty years ago in the memorable days of 1776 he had the exultation of seeing the British fleet depart, giving up to the patriot cause the City of

Boston, military key of New England, presage of the sister victory five years later on the plains of Virginian Yorktown. Massachusetts Generals gladly served under Washington, Knox, and Putnam, and a host of other officers, in the common enterprise of securing independence for a new Nation. The first great patriot victory was in Boston Harbor and the concluding victory was on the York River. At this moment your Virginian United States Attorney, General Charles Lee, sits in the cabinet with the Massachusetts Secretary of State, Timothy Pickering.

As a Massachusetts man, Sir, I cannot be denied the share of my State and of my family in that common and glorious work under the George Washington whose marble effigy stands there, whose valor and military genius made possible the independence of the United States, whose presence and influence in the recent Constitutional Convention has assured the people of every State that their liberties were safe under the New Roof, who at this moment is guiding the Ship of State in the troubled waters of desperate foreign wars, whose public duties alone make possible the acceptance of this statue without his revered presence. Were he with us today, what speaker could find the just and elegant phrases necessary to compare the man of flesh with his prototype the man of marble?

You need not be told that this is a great statue by a great artist. You realize that in future centuries pilgrims from other parts of the United States and from foreign countries will come here to acquaint themselves with what in my humble judgment is the most lifelike characterization of General George Washington, son of Virginia, General of the Continental Armies, and President of the United States.

George Washington had a brave youth full of adventure and danger and responsibility. I venture to predict that there will be in the future less authentic statues of the boy

[19]

Washington, of young Washington the undaunted messenger to the French Commander, of Washington the explorer of the western wilds. There will be statues also of Washington in the full panoply of war. Our great artist, Houdon — may his years be long and his mallet be busy, for he is one of the world's creative spirits — I predict for him a long career as one of the world's most renowned artists. Would that he were here today to be crowned with our Virginia laurel for his victories of peace. His it has been to make inert marble glow with the ineffaceable intelligence of our hero.

Speak, Washington — add your tribute to the genius of the man from overseas who knows how to give life to metal and to stone! Hail today to that wondrous artistic spirit who stood before a shapeless block and said "Washington come forth!" who can make the rocks speak, and the marks of his chisel shine with golden light. Hail to our great statue of a great American made by the hand of a great master!

Who is this Washington who stands before us? The General? Yes, but not the chief officer at the head of his troops, nor yet the foresighted commander pondering upon the dispositions of tomorrow. Do you observe that the sword is hung upon the fasces along with the military cloak? Houdon has divined the reflective Washington, the solver of problems before they become crises, the spirit whom future generations perhaps may call a mind reader of his opponent's plans. This cold marble is the graven likeness of Washington who today, while we admire his statue, is working out the problems of our national government.

At the same time this is our Washington as many of us have seen him, and as the artist saw him in his own home at Mount Vernon. It is Washington, no longer young,

Washington in his fifties, the sober, thoughtful, foresighted Washington. Is not that attitude of the head thrown back to clear the vision, one that many of you have observed? What statesman of our time in any land has looked farther into the future than George Washington? In that clear, outward gaze I read a mind which judges the future from the events of the present. What else is this statue but Washington today stepping forward into tomorrow?

Posterity will ask, upon what was the mind of Washington directed while this statue was making ready? If the speaker were a seer he would tell you what that Washington there is thinking about today in far-off Philadelphia. Three months ago, on February 15 to my knowledge, he was writing on a subject neither military nor civil. We all know that our Washington has been by profession an engineer, a builder of roads, a planner of fortifications — that he has been architect and builder of the beautiful mansion of Mount Vernon where some of you have partaken of his hospitality. Do you realize also that Washington is interested in things that to our ordinary minds seem impossible? He is known to have observed and commented hopefully upon the plans of one Rumsey for propelling boats by some kind of machinery. Would that such a thing were possible, for it would alter the conditions and enlarge the profitableness of our commerce beyond belief. So far we might go with him, but how can we accept his prognostication, as some people do, that this man Blanchard who soars into the jaws of death in the thing that he calls a balloon may be on the brink of a discovery that will be very useful to the people of the United States? So in a letter written about three months ago he characterizes as a "valuable and useful discovery" a dream of substitution of iron bridges for stone arches. I am relieved to know that the engineer mind of Washington, as reflected in the statue, hesitates to accept the proposition that an iron bridge would be cheaper than a stone bridge of the same span. There is caution in our Washington.

Washington is suffering from one cause which will die out as the Republic advances. He says with regard to the newspaper attacks upon him, with which we are unfortunately too familiar: "I have a consolation which no earthly power can deprive me of, that of acting from my best judgment; and I shall be very much mistaken, if I do not soon find that the public mind is recovering fast from the disquietude into which it has been thrown by the most willful, artful, and malignant misrepresentations that can be imagined. The current is certainly turned, and is beginning to run strong the other way."

You are all aware that the country is in the midst of a fierce political excitement hardly matched in the seven years of government under the Federal Constitution. It is only ten weeks ago since President Washington assured us that "If the people of this country have not abundant cause to rejoice at the happiness they enjoy, I know of no country that has. We have settled all our disputes, and are at peace with all nations. We supply their wants with our superfluities, and are well paid for doing so. The earth generally, for years past, has yielded its fruits bountifully. No city, town, village, or even farm but what exhibits evidences of increasing wealth and prosperity; while taxes are hardly known but in name."

At the same time, the President's mind has been bent upon those homely domestic problems which are the care and the happiness of private life. From a source which I am not at liberty to divulge, I am able to quote from a private letter written as recently as April 7, 1796, about his niece: "Harriot, having little or no fortune of her own, has no right to expect a great one in a husband; but it is desirable she should marry a gentleman, one who is well connected and can support her decently, in the life she has always moved. Otherwise she would not find matrimony, with a large family perhaps about her and scanty means, so eligible a situation as she may have conceived."

The cares of office hang heavy upon our President's head. It is a violation of no confidence that a week ago today Washington wrote to an intimate friend: "Serious misfortunes originating in misrepresentation, frequently flow, and spread, before they can be dissipated by truth. These things do, as you have supposed, fill my mind with much concern and serious anxiety. Indeed the trouble and perplexities which they occasion, added to the weight of years, which have passed over me, have worn away my mind more than my body, and render ease and retirement indispensably necessary to both, during the short time I have to stay here."

In the future history of the United States, this festival today, characterized by the profound reflections of those of you who are intrusted with the public affairs of the State and Nation, will be intimately connected with one of the most important and far-reaching communications of the President of the United States with his countrymen. It is no secret among the group of public men in closest association with the President that he has for some time had in mind a somewhat elaborate statement of his views upon public questions and his expectancy for the happy future of our beloved country. Some months ago he took counsel with certain statesmen most intimately connected with him by official relations and personal confidence.

There is a man well known as a gallant officer during the late war, for a time closely associated as a member of the General's military family, who for several years occupied a most important post in the Cabinet of the President.

By channels undoubted, though I am not at liberty to mention them, it has come to my knowledge that five days ago that eminent statesmen, Alexander Hamilton of New York, who has not the honor of the admiration and confidence of some Virginians, wrote to the President: "When last in Philadelphia, you mentioned to me your wish, that I should redress a certain paper, which you had prepared. As it is important that a thing of this kind should be done with great care, and must at leisure be touched and retouched, I submit a wish, that as soon as you have given it the body you mean it to have, it may be sent to me." On this very day, Sir, May 14, 1796, perhaps while these words are being uttered, is being dispatched from the President a letter to that statesman, who is no farther away than the City of New York, with regard to the paper which we may expect will come to be called "Washington's Farewell Address."

You, Sir, and this elegant concourse of Virginia ladies and gentlemen, will, I feel assured, as well as your children and grand-children, read those immortal words which are being considered today by the President of the United States. You can almost hear him say to the American people, "Let it always be remembered to your praise, and as an instructive example in our annals, that under circumstances in which the passions agitated in every direction were liable to mislead, amidst appearances sometimes dubious, vicissitudes of fortune often discouraging, in situations in which not unfrequently want of success has countenanced the spirit of criticism, the constancy of your support was the essential prop of the efforts, and a guarantee of the plans by which they were effected."

And again, "Profoundly penetrated with this idea, I shall carry it with me to the grave, as a strong incitement to unceasing vows that Heaven may continue to you the choicest tokens of its beneficence — that your union and brotherly affection may be perpetual — that the free constitution, which is the work of your hands, may be sacredly maintained — that its administration in every department may be stamped with wisdom and virtue — that, in fine, the happiness of the people of these States, under the auspices of liberty, may be made complete, by so careful a preservation and so prudent a use of this blessing as will acquire to them the glory of recommending it to the applause, the affection, and adoption of every nation, which is yet a stranger to it."

Doubtless in this Assemblage could be found more than one man who in Congress or in the State Legislature has expressed solicitude as to decisions of public policy made by our President. In the last three years we have all felt the disturbing influence of the foreign wars in which the former enemy Great Britain and our former allies the French are now engaged. We live in a very critical period and no man can predict safely the outcome of these desperate struggles by land and sea. Our hope is that the treaty negotiated last year by our South Carolina associate, Pinckney, will put an end to the immediate difficulties with Spain involving to some degree the interests of our daughter State, Kentucky, so recently admitted to the Union.

We of Virginia are bound to feel a special confidence and affection in our President not only because he is a son of Virginia, but because throughout his public life he has been deeply interested in that new and alluring portion of the Union which we call the West. Hear, therefore, with interest words which will be found in that momentous document when it is presented for our perusal : "The East in a like intercourse with the West, already finds, and in the progressive improvement of interior communications, by land and water, will more and more find, a valuable vent for the commodities which it brings from abroad, or

[25]

manufactures at home. The West derives from the East supplies requisite to its growth and comfort; and what is perhaps of still greater consequence, it must of necessity owe the secure enjoyment of indispensable outlets for its own productions to the weight, influence, and the future maritime strength of the Atlantic side of the Union, directed by an indissoluble community of interest, as one Nation. Any other tenure by which the West can hold this essential advantage, whether derived from its own separate strength or from an apostate and unnatural connection with any foreign power, must be intrinsically precarious."

In our secure position upon deep tidal rivers leading down to the open sea, with our opportunities of traffic by water to the sister States northward, and to the great marts of trade in Europe, we need Washington's reminder of the superior advantages of internal commerce. The trade of the new States of Kentucky and Tennessee and of the Northwest Territory, soon to become the seventeenth member of the Confederacy, is far more valuable than all that crosses the ocean in either direction. Who within this Commonwealth or outside has seen with such clearness the significance of those western regions? Need I remind this assemblage that more than forty years ago George Washington became the most important and most effective influence for holding the West as a part of the common heritage? What individual approached Washington in his influence to supplant the French in their endeavor to seize upon the valley of the Ohio and make it another Canada of rude frontiersmen closely associated with the savage inhabitants?

Who has seen, like Washington, the necessity of the early establishment of lines of communication across the mountains? Who has so urged upon the Legislature of this State and its neighboring sister Maryland the improvement of highways from the West and the reinforcement of the waterways by artificial canals? Who saw so early and so deeply as George Washington the danger that that bright star, the West, should be lost from the galaxy of the United States? When in course of time the letters and the documents of Washington bearing upon this subject are brought to public attention, we shall realize that he was the first Virginian to penetrate the western wilds under a commission emanating from the Governor of Virginia. Who strove for years to induce settlements of Virginians in what at first were but pathless wilds and in his own lifetime are becoming rich and populous states? Who first realized the significance of the Great Lakes? Who was it who ten years ago suggested a canal from the headwaters of the Mohawk to the Lakes? Who foresaw that Detroit was to be an emporium of northwestern trade? Who wrote to Lafayette at the end of the war that he had it in mind to make his way to tidewater St. Lawrence and thence up lake and river to the head of Lake Michigan and down the Illinois and the Mississippi rivers to New Orleans, and thence to return overland?

A century hence Americans will realize what it meant for the future great Republic that George Washington as pioneer, as head of the Continental Army, and as President of the United States, insisted that the regions between the Alleghenies and the Mississippi River are a rightful part of the heritage of the American people. There is still opportunity, my hearers, for a wider reach of exploration and of occupation by Virginians and by people from all the other states of the Union. We know that Washington is aware of a lonely trading post, the Lake of the Woods, somewhere far to the northwest — a carrying place between the far waters of the Mississippi and the mysterious rivers falling into the Pacific. We know that he has had in his vast mind a country called California overlooking the Pacific Ocean. Who can tell whether a few years hence another Virginia President may arise who will complete the edifice of our territorial greatness by adding that vast region of rivers, plain, and mountain which we call Louisiana. Speak, Statue! Does not thy heart bound with expectation of that greater and imperial United States stretching from ocean to ocean, and from the frozen north to the tropical coasts of the Gulf of Mexico?

Today our Jefferson, who has been at the fore for many years, stands outside the national government as critic and as prophet of disaster. It is but three weeks ago that he wrote to his Italian friend Mazzei: "The main body of our citizens, however, remain true to their republican principles; the whole landed interest is republican and so is a great mass of talents. Against us are the Executive, the Judiciary, two out of three branches of the Legislature, all the officers of the government, all who want to be officers, all timid men who prefer the calm of despotism to the boisterous sea of liberty, British merchants and Americans trading on British capital, speculators and holders in the banks and public funds. . . . In short we are likely to preserve the liberty we have obtained only by unremitting labors and perils, but we shall preserve it." Yes, Jefferson, 'tis for thee to preserve, to enlarge, and to inspire. Millions yet unborn shall practice that democracy of which thou art the prophet!

Come let us view this mineral presentment of our Washington as divined by the great artist who is making him known to future generations. All friends of the President know that he speaks of himself as six feet high. Houdon who has every incentive to be exact portrays him as six feet and two inches in height, an elevation not reached by one man in a thousand. The sculptor recognizes that Washington is no longer young, yet in the cold marble allows him the elasticity of the outdoorsman. His dress is the military. His cloak and sword he has laid on the fasces, emblem of civil power — the soldier passing to the legislator. His hair is in the familiar queue — does he carry that queue to his bed? His dress is that of a military gentleman — close coat, full pockets, ruffles, and neckcloth as he wears them, his watch seals free, a strong and muscular foot clad in boot and spur.

A hundred volumes will be written about the man and his ways, but none of them will so arouse the mind of his countrymen as this commanding expression in stone — head back, face forward, confronting the problems of his life and of his country's weal. Despite the military dress, this statue is Washington the statesman, Washington the man of affairs, Washington exemplar of character, Washington confronting and surmounting problems of his life and of his country.

* *
*

On this dedication day it is well to recall the reasons why Washington would have a statue while hundreds of his associates are rewarded with milder forms of gratitude. Let us, therefore, briefly review the reasons which were in the minds of the Virginia Legislature thirteen years ago and are in our minds today for giving him so rich and permanent a memorial. The service of the Washingtons to Virginia begins with his great-grandfather, John Washington, mariner, settler, member of the colony government, who bought the estate at Bridges Creek upon which our George was born. 'Twould be a mighty gift to Virginia if this birthplace of the man destined to be the successful commander, the first President, and the greatest American, should be made a national shrine.

His ancestors also served in various civil capacities and his half brother, Lawrence, lost health and shortened his life in the Cartagena Campaign, which was a contribution of lives and services by the Colonies to the interests of the mother country. His professional service as a surveyor, duly certified by the College of William and Mary, helped to open up a wide country to lusty settlers. At twenty-seven years of age, he became a member of the House of Delegates and continued that service down to the Revolution, one of those quiet, ineloquent, attentive members so helpful in the public business. He was present at the meeting in St. John's Church, Richmond, when Patrick Henry, later our Governor, lighted the torch with the ever memorable, "Give me liberty or give me death."

Our Washington deserves honor also for his service as the most enlightened farmer in Virginia. Future generations will recognize how far he went in advance of his agricultural brethren. What a service he performed in revealing the possibilities of selection of seeds and plants and young trees. He set up at Mount Vernon the first agricultural experiment station in the English colonies. The crying need in Virginia of today is a group of men skilled in affairs, land improvers, merchants, miners, manufacturers, clearers of the swamps. Such services became his profession. The banks that are slowly making their way throughout the Union have been aided by the participation of Washington as stockholder in Virginia banks. His hospitality and world-wide friendships have brought travelers and soldiers and statesmen from all over Europe, a service in which he shares with our former Governor, Thomas Jefferson.

The original conflict on the frontier fifty years ago was much more than a warning to the French to keep out of an unsettled region desired by the British. It was to enforce claims of the Colony of Virginia which were later amicably shared with Pennsylvania. The charter of Maryland being limited to the westward by its text, Virginia, though having lost its charter long since, carried claims and settlers far to the West. Washington received and bought land warrants in Virginia, in Pennsylvania, and in the later State of Kentucky.

Personal reward for these services to his Colony and State was not what Washington has had ultimately in mind. It is supposed that he will distribute his acquired lands and other property among kin and friends. He has already invested funds in the canal enterprises which promise so much for the future wealth of Virginia. Money rewards he has always declined. Hence the peculiar significance of our statue which expresses the good will, the admiration, and the affection of the people of this Commonwealth for the great man.

But, impetuous Virginians, perhaps you demand, "What have you, puritan dweller in the arctic regions of the United States, to do with Washington? He was born in this community and has never acknowledged citizenship elsewhere. Forty of his sixty-nine years have been spent in Virginia. His kindred are Virginians. Most of his property is in Virginia. When next year he follows out his purpose of withdrawing from public life, he will again follow the course of a Virginia gentleman's life. What have you done for Washington or what has Washington done for you to justify your presence here today?"

For myself I can but plead the mandate of the Governor of the Commonwealth combined with an unalterable purpose never to refuse the expression of allegiance and affection for George Washington of Virginia and of the United States. And I might well say, never could I forget the debt of gratitude and affection due from every

State in the Union and due in a peculiar sense from Massachusetts.

For George Washington first appeared on the Massachusetts horizon in the year 1756 as representative of the Virginia officers to protest against their subordination to the holders of British commissions however low in rank, resulting in the eventful decision that "in case it should happen that Colonel Washington and Captain Dagworthy should join at Fort Cumberland, it is my order that Colonel Washington shall take the command."

Some people in Boston remembered that visit when in 1775 General George Washington, Commander-in-Chief of the Continental Army, appeared outside the British lines before Boston. A year later came the surrender of that port, the first of Washington's victories with poorly armed and nourished Americans over the crack troops of Great Britain. Several times later has Washington made his appearance in New England, including that famous discussion with Governor John Hancock which resulted in the establishment of the principle that the President of the United States in any State outranks the Governor of any Commonwealth, even of Virginia.

Washington deserves a statue, as faithful and as spiritual as that which stands under this roof, at the hands of Massachusetts; if for nothing else, because of the friendships that he formed with Massachusetts men. John Adams proposed him for General of the Continental Army; and in this year 1796, he is a presumable candidate for the Presidency to succeed Washington. Timothy Pickering, Samuel Osgood, Henry Knox, Israel Putnam, were military or civilian subordinates. The two houses that he occupied as headquarters in Cambridge are sacred monuments. The lines that he occupied and from which he besieged the British for a year are still discernible. The main highway from Boston to Providence will in course of time be named for Washington by every town through which it runs. Every private house or hostelry which Washington visited in our State will be set apart. Arnold's daredevil expedition to Canada started from Massachusetts. The Constitution of Massachusetts drawn by John Adams sixteen years ago was recently used to advantage by the National Constitutional Convention of 1787. Both states share with Kentucky the dignity of being Commonwealths by title.

We, of Massachusetts, Sir, by high and indivisible right claim George Washington to be our countryman, our general, our statesman, our President. My prophetic eyes look forward a hundred years. Nay, why shall not, in the year 1932, the two hundredth anniversary of the birth of George Washington, the two Commonwealths each for itself and both joining with all the States old and new then in the Union, repeat today's tribute to George Washington? Our distinguished Vice-President John Adams quotes Washington's brief great speech twenty-one years ago, for which we of Massachusetts love him, "I will raise one thousand men, subsist them at my own expense, and march myself at their head for the relief of Boston."

Would, Your Excellency, that my eyes might behold that great day of celebrations. It is already ordained that the capital city of the United States shall be called Washington, but that name will much farther run. I hesitate not to predict that there will be Washingtons in many States, cities, counties, and towns, pleasure grounds and streets. The face of Washington shall everywhere be seen in reproduction of this statue and of other statues in other cities. Portraits of Washington made by the renowned artists of this time will be held more precious than gold and jewels. To possess a letter proceeding from the hand of Washington will be to own a treasure. The countenance, the services, and the character of Washington shall be known to millions of school children. His house at Mount Vernon shall be a national shrine. My prophetic mind goes farther. I see afar, in lands untrod by Washington, perhaps sloping down to the vast Pacific Ocean, a puissant State of Washington exulting in its privilege of bearing the hero's name.

Would, Your Excellency, that my mind could conceive all the vast changes of the next century and a half in fields most interesting to Washington. He is a canal builder; the Nation may live to see a ship canal within its jurisdiction extending from ocean to ocean. Washington is reaching out for some motive force more powerful than wind or river current; perhaps craft may be built which without oar or sail will voyage across oceans. Washington is a road builder; and you, here today in 1796, may live to see roads of iron traversed by vehicles of frightful speed, fifteen miles an hour, aye twenty. Washington is a manufacturer on his own estate. There will come a time when factories half a mile long will be constructed in Virginia carried on by power which we can hardly conceive. These balloons, so recently invented by the Frenchman, Montgolfier, so interesting to Washington, can we think of them as self-propelling, crossing continents and oceans?

Washington is interested in education, of children and of youth. Might we suppose that in Virginia and in other States will arise great universities with instructors and students numerous enough to make a town, developing fields of study yet undreamed? The United States has shown itself a power that must be dealt with as a free and self-protecting nation. Can we imagine the carrying out of the hopes and aspirations of Washington, that ours shall one day be the most powerful, the most widely educated, and richest of all the nations in the world?

Ours is a broad country with a majestic coast line, a rich and fertile belt of settlements near the coast. I have already spoken of vast possibilities of expansion and mighty fields of political power. Too recent has been our experience of the difficulties and the horrors and the sacrifices of war. We desire peace with all the world. Yet, methinks it not impossible that within two years from now the rapidly changing kaleidoscope of European affairs may bring our country into such danger that Washington, retired from office, will be called upon again to give his military counsel on preparations for war. As President he has already shown himself interested in a national navy; and who knows how soon a federal frigate *Constitution* may prove that the dormant navy can revive?

America is not yet in equilibrium. Our President is facing the question of the Mississippi, and particularly of the outlet of the West by that river to the Gulf of Mexico. We may foresee ultimate extension to Florida, the region in which Washington once sought a tract of land. At this moment the counselors of the Executive are facing the great question whether the United States can show power and vitality enough to protect its own interests on the sea. Gentlemen of Virginia, you share with Massachusetts and with every State now in the Union or hereafter to be admitted, in these great questions which are sure to arise, which tax the ability of our Washington, and will tax the abilities of some President a century, aye a century and a half, in the future.

This building and its contents have not escaped the attention and interest of the foreign travelers who since the end of the war have visited our country and have published many accounts of their observations. Only four years ago came to this city and to this building, the Duke de La Rochefoucault Liancourt, a Frenchman of rank and literary aspirations, who stood on that spot yonder. First with pleasure he observed this magnificent Capitol which reminded him of one of the most beautiful survivals of Roman architecture. "The Capitol," he writes, in words now translated into English, "is erected on a point of this hill which commands the town. This edifice, which is extremely vast, is constructed on the plan of the *Maison Carée*, at Nîmes, but on a much more extensive scale. The attics of the *Maison Carée* have undergone an alteration in the Capitol, to suit them for the convenience of the public offices of every denomination, which, thus perfectly secure against all accidents from fire, lie within reach of the tribunals, the executive council, the governor, the general assembly, who all sit in the Capitol and draw to it a great afflux of people. This building, which is entirely of brick, is not yet coated with plaster: the columns, the pilasters, are destitute of bases and capitals; but the interior and exterior cornices are finished, and are well executed. The rest will be completed with more or less speed; but, even in its present unfinished state, this building is, beyond comparison, the finest, the most noble, and the greatest, in all America. The internal distribution of its parts is extremely well adapted to the purposes for which it is destined. It was Mr. Jefferson who, during his embassy in France, sent the model of it. Already it is said to have cost a hundred and seventy thousand dollars; and fifteen thousand more are the estimated sum requisite for completing it and remedying some defects which have been observed in the construction."

Liancourt, who was here in Richmond but a few months ago, failed to appreciate the artistic completeness of the statue which we are here to dedicate. "In the great central vestibule," says he, "which is lighted by a kind of dome contained in the thickness of the roof, has lately been placed a statue of George Washington, voted, ten years since, by the General Assembly of Virginia. In addition to the sentiments of gratitude which they felt in common with the rest of America, that body entertained moreover a particular affection for him, together with the pride of having him for their countryman. Since that period the President has acquired new claims to the general approbation and esteem. If he be chargeable with some errors in administration, as I think he is, nevertheless his devotion to the public weal and the purity of his intentions cannot even be suspected; yet it is doubtful whether at the present moment the Assembly of Virginia would be inclined to vote him such an honor — at least it is certain that the same unanimity would not prevail on the occasion. This statue was executed by Houdon, one of the first sculptors in France. He undertook a voyage to America five or six years since for the express purpose of making a bust of the President from the life. Although the statue be beautiful, and display even a nobleness in the composition and a likeness in the features, it does not bear the marks of Houdon's talent: one cannot trace in it the hand of him who produced the celestial Diana which constitutes the chief part of that artist's reputation.

"Near this statue of the president stands a marble bust of *Monsieur* de Lafayette, voted at the same time by the Assembly of Virginia, and also carved by Houdon."

Great Washington, not from us, thy countrymen, proceeds so unapt a judgment. What! shall an alien, a visitor, a passing macaroni, instil into the minds of Washington's countrymen sentiments so faint? We have seen thee, we have listened to thee. We hold thee here as thou art in the flesh. Thus have we loved thee! So let us love this lifelike image. Washington, stand forth from this marble! Thou canst not speak, yet we all but hear thy voice. Stand forth, Washington, to bless, to remind, and to inspire thy countrymen. And not Virginians only, for this image in marble will bring home to the minds of millions of future Americans that ardent, that exalted, that fatherly love for his countrymen which speaks to us today through the lips of this great statue of the Greatest American.

The minutes swiftly pass and still Washington waits for us to complete this survey of what his statue represents, in experience, in power, in patriotism, in influence on the future. Never shall we see another Washington, for he is the rarest product of an age of giants and of giant tasks. There may be many Virginia born Governors of this Commonwealth, and perchance a succession of future Presidents of our United States will in the years to come spring from this nursery of statesmen ; but there is only one Washington and this statue is his habitation.

Yet as a northern man, I seem to see far in the future a figure unborn this year 1796. He shall be descended of a Massachusetts family which has become a Pennsylvania family and then a Virginia family. He shall be a son and grandson of native Virginians, born himself in Kentucky, which till four years ago was an outlying district of Virginia. Not at the battle front against Indians or British, yet commander-in-chief of more troops than ever participated in all American wars before his time. I seem to see far in the future a President who, like Washington, is a man of peace and like Washington a man of war. To my prophetic mind arises the Virginian, Abraham Lincoln. In that far future he will arise like Washington, proud of his State, yet like Washington loving the Union of all States above any State. I can foresee that man as so admiring Washington that in the earliest notable address of his life, fifty years hence, he will utter these glowing words as a tribute to the original of our statue : "And that we improved to the last, that we remained free to the last, that we revered his name to the last, that during his long sleep we permitted no hostile foot to pass over or desecrate his resting-place, shall be that which to learn when the last trump shall awaken our Washington. Upon these let the proud fabric of freedom rest, as the rock of its basis."

THOMAS JEFFERSON

President of the United States

1801–1809

The Honorable JOHN W. DAVIS, The Speaker

FROM THE INTRODUCTION OF THE SPEAKER
by
GOVERNOR POLLARD

We are met today to do honor to the memory of another great Virginian. These are not idle ceremonies. We are not here to indulge our pride in our forefathers — we are here to renew our allegiance to the great principles for which they fought. True we are reaching back into the history of the past, but we are not wasting our time rummaging for relics, we are emphasizing living principles.

[43]

Jefferson, the man we honor today, was the greatest political philosopher of his age. Of all the wonderful sentiments which came from his heart and mind there is one which grips the liberty-loving soul as none other. It is this, "I have sworn on the altar of God eternal hostility against every form of tyranny over the mind of man." His hostility was against every form of tyranny

ATTILIO PICCIRILLI, *The Sculptor*

over the mind. There was a tyranny of law now happily passed away; but there remains today in all its cruelty a tyranny which proscribes, ostracizes, denounces, and condemns those who dare to think for themselves. The spirit of liberty of thought will never be completely enthroned until men have a more generous regard for those who differed with them. This is an ideal of Jefferson not yet realized but towards which we, his followers, may continue to labor.

Jefferson made many contributions to the political thought of his day; but he will stand out in history as the chief exponent of religious liberty, which is America's distinctive contribution to the science of government.

Jefferson sent ringing down through the ages the immortal truth that all men are "free to profess and by argument to maintain their

JEAN TILLIER, *Chairman, Committee of French Citizens, The Donors*

*opinions in matters of religion, and that the same shall in no wise
diminish, enlarge, or affect their civil capacities."*

*In selecting the orator for each of these occasions, I have sought
to choose the one who most nearly represented the ideals of the
Statesman we were to honor. There is no greater living exponent
of the principles of Thomas Jefferson than John W. Davis, sound
and brilliant student of the Constitution, once the standard bearer
of the party which Jefferson founded.*

[45]

THOMAS JEFFERSON

ADDRESS BY

THE HONORABLE JOHN W. DAVIS

IN the Capitol of the State of Virginia we come to place a bust of the second of Virginia's sons who reached the Presidency of the United States. That it is the gift of citizens of France, a nation which he so truly admired, adds grace and distinction to the event. Washington alone excepted, this third President of the United States is better known to history than any other Virginian; and Washington again excepted, he rendered to his State and Nation more distinguished service than any man ever born on Virginia soil. Indeed, in the chosen field of Jefferson's labors he stands as preëminent as does Washington, still in my humble judgment the greatest of all Americans, in his. Without the sword of Washington the American Nation could hardly have come into being, and without the pen of Jefferson it might not have found its soul. A Virginian of the Virginians in every nerve and fiber, he was equally an American of the Americans. While, at the same time, his far-ranging interest in human affairs and in the history, art, literature, and science of other peoples entitled him to be called in the best sense a citizen of the world. To the Presidency he brought the most informed and comprehensive intellect that ever adorned that office, and, by common consent, he stamped his ideas and personality upon his contemporaries and upon succeeding generations to an extent unrivaled by any other American statesman. It is not too much to say that the political and social life of America is what it is today in large part because of the teachings and the labors of Thomas Jefferson. While the occasion makes it fitting to inquire what manner of man he was of whom these things can be said, it is surely unnecessary in this presence to do more than give the barest outline of his career. He was born the son of a frontier farmer in Albemarle County, Virginia, on the second day of April, old style, the thirteenth by the present calendar, in the year 1743. He died within sight of his birthplace on the fourth day of July, 1826, in the eighty-fourth year of his life. As he lay waiting for the summons of the Final Messenger, his dying memory ran back over half a century and, ignoring many scenes in which he had played a part, fixed itself upon the great event that had transpired just fifty years before. His last audible words were, "Is this the Fourth?"

After two years of industrious study at William and Mary College, he read law under George Wythe, that "incarnation of justice," whom he was later, when Governor of Virginia and Visitor of William and Mary, to install as the first occupant of a chair of law in any American college. He was introduced to the bar by that faithful preceptor and friend in 1767 and enjoyed seven years of busy and successful practice. At the end of that time, as the clouds of the Revolution gathered, he was compelled to abandon his profession forever under the growing demand for his services in public life. The first public offices conferred upon him were those of Justice of the Peace of Albemarle County and Vestryman of his native parish in the year 1764. The last was that of Rector of the University of Virginia, which he held at the time of his death. During the intervening years he was a member of the House of Burgesses of the Colony of Virginia, a Delegate of Virginia in the Continental Congress, a Member of the Virginia Assembly, Governor of the State, twice elected to the Congress of the United States, Minister Plenipotentiary to France, first Secretary of State of the United States, Vice-President, and twice elected to the Presidency.

At one time or another he was a farmer, a lawyer, a legislator, a revolutionary, a diplomat, a parliamentarian, an executive, an inventor, a musician, a sociologist, a botanist, an astronomer, a paleontologist, an architect, a mechanic, a philologist, a landscape gardener, a linguist, an author, a party leader and politician, and withal a profound political philosopher. In every public or private station that he filled, his many-sided intellect made its mark, and as each new opportunity presented itself he turned it to permanent and lasting account. From his earliest manhood to the day of his death, at home or abroad — whether building and beautifying Monticello, revising the laws of his State, organizing committees of correspondence among the revolting colonies, writing for the judgment of mankind the roster of their wrongs, laboring to remove the restrictions on American commerce, giving to the Senate its parliamentary code, devising a decimal currency for the new Nation, purchasing an empire for the Union, creating a party to do battle for the social order in which he believed, or laying with his own hands the foundations of the University of Virginia — he was always and everywhere a builder. An idealist, a dreamer if you choose, he yet had the priceless gift of knowing how to make his dreams come true. So durable, indeed, are the things he built, whether in the world of matter or of spirit, that after the storms of a century to find his monument one need but look around.

His own appraisal of his activities we have in the self-composed epitaph that adorns his tombstone:

AUTHOR OF THE
DECLARATION OF AMERICAN INDEPENDENCE
OF THE
STATUTE OF VIRGINIA FOR RELIGIOUS FREEDOM
AND FATHER OF THE
UNIVERSITY OF VIRGINIA

By these, as "testimonials that he had lived, he wished most to be remembered" — this was the picture of himself he desired the coming years to gaze upon. And to these simple words he wished nothing to be added beyond the naked dates of his birth and death. It was a sure and certain bid for immortality. To add to or subtract from it now would seem an act of gross impiety. And yet history cannot be forced to satisfy itself with this brief catalogue of his life's results, and posterity is entitled to its own judgment of the relative importance of the things he did. Certain it is that in the scales of time his weight can still be felt, for touch American life where you will, in law, in politics, in education, in diplomacy, or in statecraft, the influence of Jefferson appears. Well may one ask what subtle attribute it is that gives his personality this pervasive and enduring force.

He wrote the Declaration of Independence. Franklin and Adams, Roger Sherman and Robert Livingston were his colleagues on the committee appointed to prepare it, but the thing was done by him in the seclusion of his own closet. Except for some minor matters of form and the elimination by Congress of that attack upon the slave trade, to which Jefferson so often returned, the document stands today as it came from his pen. He did not come as a stranger to the task, for his "Summary View of the Rights of British America," which he had prepared for the Virginian Convention, had not only won attention at home but had procured him the honor of having his name enrolled in a bill of attainder designed for the British Parliament. His specific and terrible indictment of the British King and his government was read from every pulpit and on every hustings, and it rang throughout the country like a fire bell in the night. It steeled the hearts of the scattered colonists for the trials they were to undergo and served notice on England and the world of the determination with which they were inspired. Yet if that had been all the Declaration contained, it would have gone into history after its immediate task was over to find a high and honorable place among other revolutionary manifestoes and nothing more. But its author seized the opportunity to render it a living force by embodying in its preamble in a few terse and nervous sentences the triple ideals of human equality, personal liberty, and popular sovereignty to which the new Nation was to be dedicated; ideals that have marched with it ever since as the pillar of cloud by day and of fire by night throughout its pilgrimage. "We hold these truths to be self-evident," he wrote; and no man since has dared openly to challenge them before an American audience.

He wrote the "Statute of Virginia for Religious Freedom." It was a long step forward in an age when statute books were loaded with religious discrimination and odious pains and penalties were visited upon the non-conformist. Today, even though religious rancor may still raise at times its loathsome head, it is nevertheless, thanks to Jefferson, a commonplace of American thought that "No man shall be compelled to frequent or support any religious worship, place, or ministry whatsoever, nor shall be enforced, restrained, molested, or burdened in his body or goods, nor shall otherwise suffer, on account of his religious opinions or beliefs; but that all men shall be free to profess and by argument to maintain their opinions in matters of religion, and that the same shall in no wise diminish, enlarge, or affect their civil capacities." Yet here again the author of this statute, in the flaming language of its preamble, made its vindication rest secure upon the assertion that freedom of opinion is divinely granted and therefore not subject to any civil control, and that freedom of speech and of argument are the all-sufficient weapons of truth.

He founded the University of Virginia, breaking new ground to make an institution of higher learning the capstone and pinnacle of an educational system supported by the State. "We owed it," said he, in speaking of its founding, "to do not what was to perish with ourselves, but what would remain to be respected and preserved through other ages." How well that hope has been realized the high place which the University of Virginia has always held in the educational world will amply testify. Yet it stands today surrounded by so great a sisterhood of similar institutions, both publicly supported and privately endowed, that the lonely eminence of other days is no longer its own. But it still cherishes as a priceless heritage the fact that it was based by its founder on "the illimitable freedom of the human mind." It was he who made it the citadel of academic freedom — freedom of teaching to the professor, freedom of study for the student, and freedom of conduct for both under an honor system which abolished the labor and the ignominy of academic espionage. It was he who gave it in charge to expound "a sound spirit of legislation, which, banishing all arbitrary and unnecessary restraint on individual action, shall leave us free to do whatever does not violate the equal rights of another" ; and he who chose its proud motto — "Ye shall know the truth and the truth shall make you free."

One after another as the works of Jefferson pass in historical review, this love of freedom will be seen to animate them all. At the very threshold of his public career he struck the mightiest blow ever delivered in America against an aristocratic caste by his bills abolishing entails and primogeniture in the State of Virginia. With prophetic eye he foresaw the perils with which human slavery threatened his country — since "God is just and His justice cannot sleep forever." Far in advance of those by whom he was surrounded, he declared himself against the institution and offered to Virginia a statute providing for its gradual and peaceful abolition. The Legislature of the State followed him so far as to forbid the importation of slaves after 1778, but public sentiment unhappily rejected the bolder course of gradual emancipation. When he drafted the Ordinance for the Government of the Northwest Territory, he inserted a provision forbidding slavery within its area after the year 1800. Ah, had Virginia been willing to consider his wise proposal, and had not Congress, by a naked majority of one, defeated the clause he wrote into the Northwest Ordinance who can say that the influence of these examples might not have been sufficient to remove in peace the cause of the "irrepressible conflict," without the shedding of fraternal blood.

The same liberty of action which he coveted for the individual he planned for the Nation. Much of his public service was devoted to an effort to remove the restrictions with which American commerce was burdened by the mercantile policy that prevailed throughout the world. When he purchased Louisiana from Napoleon, the negotiations were directed in the first place to securing freedom of commerce on the Mississippi River, with a free port of entry under American control at its mouth. When the entire domain was offered, he grasped it not through lust of territorial expansion but to liberate his country from the dread of an over-powerful neighbor on her western border. The expedition sent out under Lewis and Clarke to give us a foothold on the Pacific that finally ripened into title was but part of the same grand design.

In the political battles that preceded and followed his elevation to the Presidency, the ideal of a democratic freedom was always to the fore. He believed that the Ship of State was drifting toward the old course of aristocracy and privilege and he grasped the helm to bring her back to the line marked out by the simple phrases of the Declaration. He assumed the task of formulating the creed of American democracy, and having formulated it, he wrote its tenets on his banner and carried them to victory. It is a shallow view of history which sees the long duel between himself and Hamilton as a mere clash of incompatible personalities and ambitions. It went deeper far than that. It was but another episode in the struggle between two schools of thought that have contended with each other since the world was young: the aristocrat against the democrat; the authoritarian whose god is order and whose reliance is power against the libertarian whose passion is freedom and whose hope is in liberty; the conservative who instinctively distrusts human nature and seeks to bind it down from mischief by the chains of the law; and the liberal, who believes that law is but public sentiment made vocal and that man's better impulses can be trusted to prevail. In this clash of ideas the place of Jefferson with his passion for liberty was fore-ordained.

With such force and clarity were his views expounded that, although one may disagree with him, it is impossible to misunderstand. In this he had trained himself from youth, adopting as his motto "never to use two words where one would do"; and it is by reason both of form and substance that none of the vigor of his maxims has departed with the passing years. As Lincoln wrote, the "principles of Jefferson are the definitions and axioms of free society." They still do so remain.

The God who gave us life gave us liberty at the same time. The inherent and inalienable rights of man are unchangeable. Every man and every body of men on earth possess the right of self-government. If man cannot be trusted to govern himself, can he be trusted to govern others? It is not true that some men are born into the world with saddles on their backs while others are born booted and spurred to ride them legitimately by the grace of God. The foundation of republican government is the equal right of every citizen in his person, in his property, and in their management. Its essence is action by the citizens on matters within their right and competence and in all others by representatives chosen for that purpose. The inconveniences attending too much liberty are better than those attending too small a degree of it. Education is the only sure foundation for the preservation of freedom and happiness. Our country is too large to have all its affairs directed by a single government, and it is of immense consequence that the States retain as complete authority as possible over their own citizens. Equal and exact justice to all men, of whatever state or persuasion, religious or political. A wise and frugal government, which shall restrain men from injuring one another, shall leave them free to regulate their own pursuits of industry and improvement, and shall not take from the mouth of labor the bread it has earned — this is the sum of good government.

These sentences are among his teachings. Glittering generalities — yes, perhaps, but the light that glances from them is reflected down the ages. A tissue of abstractions, do you say? Well, even so, there runs through all the weaving like a thread of purest gold the faith of a great soul in the worth and dignity of each individual man. In this faith is the essence of Jefferson's philosophy; here is the main-spring of his every action; here the inspiration of his entire life; and here the secret of his lasting influence on the lives of other men. It is this faith by which the mountains of caste and prejudice and privilege are moved, and before which tyranny and oppression well may tremble. Armed with such weapons as Jefferson forged lovers of freedom can still go forth in this faith conquering and to conquer. For this is his supreme service to his countrymen: that he gave them their social and, in the truest sense, their political creed. When democracy as a form of government is broadly challenged, as it is today; when those who thirst for power or place or privilege seek to intrench them-selves behind unequal laws; when centralization in govern-ment threatens to strangle the rights of the citizen in its bureaucratic coils; when misguided virtue strives to make others virtuous by hedging them about with interdictions and restraints; when economy in the disbursement of public revenues is forgotten in a mad scramble for govern-mental bounty — those who have the heart and mind to do battle on the other side can turn and turn again to Jefferson and his teachings and gather new strength and courage for the unending combat.

When his spirit had returned to the God who gave it, his disciple Madison wrote, "He lives and will live in the memory and gratitude of the wise and good as a luminary of science, as a votary of liberty, as a model of patriotism, and as a benefactor of mankind." We do not dare to rewrite his epitaph, but we can invite those who gaze upon the bust erected here to recognize in him the greatest among American political philosophers, the chief among the apos-tles of freedom, the foremost liberal of the modern world.

JAMES MADISON

President of the United States

1809–1817

The Honorable *CHARLES EVANS HUGHES*, *The Speaker*

FROM THE INTRODUCTION OF THE SPEAKER

by

GOVERNOR POLLARD

The public career of James Madison began at Williamsburg as a member of the Virginia Convention of 1776. It ended in 1830 here in this Hall where he served as a member of Virginia's second Constitutional Convention.

In 1776 we find Madison, then a timid young man, twenty-five years of age, lately graduated from Princeton, taking part in the making of Virginia's first Constitution containing that immortal

[59]

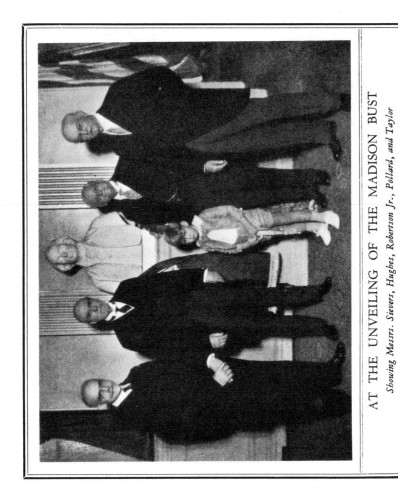

AT THE UNVEILING OF THE MADISON BUST

Showing Messrs. Sievers, Hughes, Robertson Jr., Pollard, and Taylor

Declaration of Rights destined profoundly to affect the political thought of liberty-loving people throughout the world.

Fifty-four years later, in 1830, Madison, then a man of seventy-eight, broken in health, stood upon this floor where his feeble voice was heard within these four walls in his last public utterance dealing with the principles of representative government.

The interest of this occasion is therefore enhanced because of the sacred place in which we meet.

F. WILLIAM SIEVERS, *The Sculptor*

But the occasion has an added interest because the speaker of the day presides over the deliberations of the Supreme Court of the United States, a body created by the Federal Constitution, in the making of which Madison had so prominent a part. It is fitting that the Chief Justice of that great tribunal should be here with us today to interpret the life of the man who has so often been called the Father of the Constitution.

Of Chief Justice Hughes it may be said that he holds a unique place in the affections of the American people. The admiration and esteem in which he is held is not limited by sectional, class, or party lines. He is universally respected for his character, his ability, his patriotism, and the soundness of his judgment.

JAQUELIN P. TAYLOR, *The Donor*

I now present Mr. Jaquelin P. Taylor, kinsman of President Madison, a patron of art and a devoted Virginian, through whose generosity the Commonwealth acquires title to this precious piece of marble. Mr. Taylor also was the generous donor of the bust of another of his kinsmen, President Zachary Taylor.

* *
*

I now present Mr. F. William Sievers, our own Virginia sculptor, of whose genius this beautiful bust is a product. As Governor of Virginia I am proud that we have living within our borders a sculptor whose works are well known throughout the country.

[62]

JAMES MADISON

ADDRESS BY

The Honorable CHARLES EVANS HUGHES

A s we approach the two-hundredth anniversary of the
birth of Washington, our thought is directed, not
simply to his own incomparable career, but also to the essential collaboration in statecraft which crowned the
success of Revolution. We owe our institutions to the
operation of two forces — the pressure for unity and
national power which made possible a strong Republic,
and a passion for individual liberty, which was jealous of
strength and insistent upon the protection of what were
regarded as fundamental rights. Two types of leadership
appear reflecting the devotion of rare political genius to the
one or the other of these aims. It is the unsurpassed
distinction of Virginia, not only that from her soil sprang
so many eminent statesmen of the formative period, but
that she brought each of these types to the highest point
of development, finding their historic illustration in
George Washington and John Marshall, in Patrick Henry
and Thomas Jefferson. Another personality, in whose
honor we are met today, stands out as conspicuously
exhibiting a blend of ideals and purposes, fitting him to
receive the confidence of Washington and the intimate
friendship of Jefferson, with a constructive ability and
aptitude for conciliation which in the supreme test won

for him the deserved and distinctive title of the Father of the Constitution.

James Madison began his public life in the Virginia Convention of 1776, at the age of twenty-five, and continued it with but slight interruption until he left the Presidency, forty-one years later, to enjoy the retirement of an experienced political philosopher. In the picture of that long public career, there are lights and shades. In the effort to arrest attention by novel and sensational emphasis, there is often observed a tendency to resort to biographical distortion by making a parade of mistakes and frailties. While historic accuracy is always desirable, a sense of proportion is quite as essential to a veracious narrative as familiarity with details. Much of the work of men in public life is inevitably concerned with issues and conflicts, which, although they seem to be of transcendent importance at the time, rapidly give place to other controversies and have but little permanent influence. Other labors are of a monumental character, revealing the genius of leadership and conferring lasting benefits. We are thinking today of such achievements.

I shall not abuse the privileges of this occasion by an attempt — futile, indeed, it would be — to make a comprehensive review of Madison's career, embracing his activities in the new government, as party leader in the Congress, as Secretary of State, and as President, and involving an examination of the strife of parties, the diplomatic difficulties culminating in war, the humiliations and victories of that war, and the circumstances of the ensuing peace. Important as are these events in the history of the period, their consideration should not be permitted to detract from our paramount interest in the outstanding work of Madison in laying the foundations of the Republic. In this brief tribute, I present to you

Madison in the distinction of his greatest service, as an architect of institutions and a defender of liberty.

Of the illustrious Virginians to whose public service the Nation is indebted, three were preëminent in establishing our Federal Constitution, Washington, Madison, and Marshall. Washington not only won opportunity by his military success, but made the Constitution possible by presiding at the Philadelphia Convention and giving to the issue of its labors the essential support of his great influence. "A Confederation," John Quincy Adams said, "is not a country." And in the truest sense Washington became the Father of his Country as a Nation equipped with the requisite authority of national government. At a later day, Marshall made this authority secure by his judicial exposition of cardinal constitutional principles. But both the inspiring leadership of Washington and the juristic skill of Marshall depended on the development and formulation of the constitutional scheme. In that supremely important enterprise, Madison had the leading part.

He was well equipped for the task by temperament, studies, and political experience. Cool, cautious, deliberative, he was capable of prolonged concentration in intellectual work, which resulted in convictions securely based in profound study and adequate reflection. His mental equilibrium was not upset by gusts of passion and he had no aptitude for attempts to sway others by tempestuous eloquence. He sought to convince, and he became formidable in debate because he was thorough in preparation and precise in statement. With his regard for the processes of reason, there was no acerbity in his disposition, and there was a notable absence of any assumption of superiority. Exceptionally modest, he was tolerant in spirit, temperate in speech, and conciliatory in action.

In his studies he was his own best preceptor, and he was driven by an insatiable desire for knowledge. When we reflect upon the slender scholastic opportunities of his day, we must not overlook the advantage of a student life unencumbered by a bewildering multiplicity of activities which absorb the energies of youth, too frequently at the expense of intellectual interests. Nor was the ambitious student embarrassed by a host of attractive courses and a superabundance of material leading to a dissipation of effort. We are told that Madison's favorite studies at Princeton were the history of the free states of antiquity and all subjects relating to government; and, despite the handicap of delicate health, his unremitting industry won for him the reputation of being the "deepest student" in college. Perhaps it was in the informal association of undergraduates in the American Whig Society, which he organized, that he found the most helpful discipline in the preparation of papers and in earnest debates upon government. After leaving college he continued his intellectual pursuits at home, and he brought to his public career a comprehensive knowledge of ancient and modern history which has been described as "quite unequaled among the Americans of the Revolutionary period."

With all his calmness and studiousness, he was not destitute of zeal. He had the zeal of a liberal mind. This became apparent at the very outset when, as a delegate to the State Convention which framed the constitution of Virginia, he became the champion of religious liberty, a cause to which he was devoted throughout his life. A deeply religious man, he wished religion to flourish in a free atmosphere, without leaning upon the support of government with the consequent dangers of governmental interference. Freedom of conscience in his view was a fundamental right, and it was his amendment which led

[66]

to the substitution for the words "fullest toleration," the provision that "All men are equally entitled to the free exercise of religion according to the dictates of conscience." He would have gone even further than the Convention by prohibiting emoluments and privileges on account of religion. Eight years later in the Virginia Legislature he determinedly opposed the assessment bill for the support of churches, and as the result of the response to his "Remonstrance" sent broadcast through the State, the proposed resolution was defeated, Jefferson's bill of 1779 was revived and passed, and the cause of religious liberty in Virginia had a lasting triumph. Her example was influential in other States, and Madison takes his place with Roger Williams and Thomas Jefferson in the front rank of those to whom we are indebted for the American conception of the essential freedom of the spirit from governmental license or restraint.

After his first brief term in the State Legislature, Madison was sent in 1780 as a Representative of Virginia to the Continental Congress, and his experience there gave him an intimate knowledge of the perils of Independence in the absence of Union. He put the case pithily in these words: "The close of the war brought no cure for the public embarrassments. The States, relieved from the pressure of foreign danger and flushed with the enjoyment of independent and sovereign power (instead of a diminished disposition to part with it), persevered in omissions and in measures incompatible with their relations to the Federal Government and with those among themselves." With his keen realization of pressing need, it was natural that Madison should have joined earnestly in the effort to "form a more perfect Union." In describing the genesis of the Federal Convention, Madison tells us of his own important part while not withholding the credit due to others who were seeking the same end. "The change in our government," he said,[1] "like most other important improvements ought to be ascribed rather to a series of causes than to any particular and sudden one, and to the participation of many rather than to the efforts of a single agent. It is certain that the general idea of revising and enlarging the scope of the federal authority, so as to answer the necessary purposes of the Union, grew up in many minds, and by natural degrees, during the experienced inefficacy of the old confederation. The discernment of General Hamilton must have rendered him an early patron of the idea. . . . In common with others, I derived from my service in the old Congress during the later stages of the Revolutionary War, a deep impression of the necessity of invigorating the federal authority. I carried this impression with me into the Legislature of Virginia." The fact of greatest importance is that out of Madison's efforts in that legislature grew the resolution in 1785 for the appointment of commissioners to meet at Annapolis "in order to form some plan for investing Congress with the regulation and taxation of commerce." Madison adds that "Although the step taken by Virginia was followed by the greater number of the States, the attendance at Annapolis was so tardy and so deficient, that nothing was done on the subject immediately committed to the meeting. The consultations took another turn." These resulted in the recommendation for the meeting in Philadelphia. As to this recommendation, Madison says : "The manner in which this idea rose into effect makes it impossible to say with whom it more particularly originated. I do not even recollect the member who first proposed it to the body. I have an indistinct impression that it received its first formal suggestion from Mr. Abraham Clark of New Jersey. Mr. Hamilton was certainly the

[1] *Letters to Noah Webster*, Oct. 12, 1804; March 10, 1826.

[68]

member who drafted the address." Madison then observes that the Legislature of Virginia was the first "that had an opportunity of taking up the recommendation, and the first that concurred in it. It was thought proper to express its concurrence in terms that would give the example as much weight and effect as possible; and with the same view to include in the deputation, the highest characters in the State, such as the Governor and Chancellor. The same policy led to the appointment of General Washington, who was put at the head of it."

The bill complying with the recommendation from Annapolis was written by Madison. This action was followed by appointments from other States, and finally, on February 21, 1787, the Congress passed what Madison called its "Recommendatory Resolution" giving, in effect, its sanction to the project of a Federal Convention to revise the Articles of Confederation. This removed the suspense which Congressional inaction had created. Thus the labors of Madison at last found fruition. Without his sagacity and persistence there would have been no Federal Constitution.

It is pleasant to picture this quiet and studious young man of thirty-six as he takes his place with the distinguished Virginia delegation in that body of eminent men who were to frame the political structure of the new Nation. That he fully recognized the significance of the meeting, and his remarkable forethought, are apparent from the arrangement that he at once made to secure an appropriate record of its proceedings. "The curiosity I had felt," he said, "during my researches into the history of the most distinguished confederacies, particularly those of antiquity, and the deficiency I found in the means of satisfying it . . . determined me to preserve as far as I could an exact account of what might pass in the Convention whilst executing its trust, with the magnitude of which I was duly impressed. . . . I chose a seat in front of the presiding member, with the other members on my right and left hands. In this favorable position for hearing all that passed, I noted in terms legible and in abbreviations and marks intelligible to myself what was read from the chair, or spoken by the members. . . . It happened, also, that I was not absent a single day, nor more than a casual fraction of an hour in any day, so that I could not have lost a single speech unless a very short one." It was not until 1840 that this *Journal* of Madison was published and to him we owe the most important document of the period. It is not the least of his services that he thus has given us the most direct approach to the intention of the makers of the Constitution.

But the calling of a convention and the reporting its proceedings, after all, derive their importance from the action which the convention takes. What was needed was not merely a feeling of urgent need, but a *plan* adequate to solve the most pressing problems and reasonable enough to triumph over the seriously divergent views of men and states. Leadership naturally fell to Virginia which had first adopted the recommendation of the Annapolis Convention and appointed delegates. And that Virginia was ready to assume the responsibilities of leadership, and again to justify it, was undoubtedly due in the main to Madison. He had a plan. It was called the Virginia Plan, and it was the first presented to the Federal Convention. It was fittingly presented by Edmund Randolph, the Governor of the State and the head of its delegation. While the plan was appropriately developed in consultation among the Virginia delegates, Madison has been recognized as its principal author. Randolph himself wrote, "Before my departure for the Convention, I believed that the Confederation was not so eminently defective as it had been supposed." It was in the consultations which followed his arrival that Randolph reached the conclusion that a more thorough-going plan was needed, and with the knowledge of Madison's views, one can readily understand his share in producing the final conviction. The Virginia Plan was taken as a basis for the debates in the Convention. While many of its important provisions were altered in the process of making the Constitution, it had the root idea of national government operating directly upon the people and not simply upon the States, that is, as Madison explained, "national with regard to the *operation* of its powers," although limited in "the *extent* of its powers." The basic proposal of the Virginia Plan was "that a National Legislature, a National Executive, and a National Judiciary, should be established." In thus providing for national power, supreme within its sphere, for a national legislature which should make laws binding upon the people as a whole in the same manner as the laws of the State within its sphere bound the people of the State, the plan went to the heart of the existing evils. It is not extravagant to say, as John Fiske has said, that "this was the supreme act of creative statesmanship which made our country what it is," and that "it is to Madison we owe this grand and luminous conception of the two co-existing and harmonious spheres of government." Neither the important modifications of the plan, nor the compromises which were necessary to secure the adoption of the Constitution, disturbed this central principle, which today no less than heretofore makes possible the government of a vast territory with a distribution of power adapted to the satisfaction of both national and local needs. In this fundamental respect Madison stands forth as the chief architect of our political structure.

I cannot undertake to dwell upon the proceedings of the Convention, but Madison's contribution consisted not only in a plan but in his effective participation in the debates. He brought to the Convention not only exceptional learning but cogency in argument. He made one hundred and sixty-one speeches — a number exceeded only by Gouverneur Morris and James Wilson. The impression made by Madison upon his colleagues is thus described by William Pierce, a delegate from Georgia : "Every person seems to acknowledge his greatness. He blends together the profound politician with the scholar. In the management of every great question he evidently took the lead in the Convention, and though he cannot be called an orator, he is a most agreeable, eloquent, and convincing speaker. From a spirit of industry and application which he possesses in a most eminent degree, he always comes forward the best informed man of any point in debate. The affairs of the United States, he perhaps, has the most correct knowledge of, of any man in the Nation."

Mr. Pierce also refers to Madison's "remarkable sweet temper," and the Convention profited by his practical judgment as well as by his tenacity of conviction. One of the compromises of the Constitution was that relating to the apportionment of representatives in the Congress on the basis of population, embracing the whole number of free persons and three-fifths of the slaves, was a contribution of Madison, following the clause of a proposal made by him, and adopted by the Continental Congress in 1783, as a recommendation for an amendment of the Articles of Confederation. Despite the criticism to which this compromise was subsequently subjected, there can be no doubt that without it the formation of a national government with adequate authority would have been impossible. It should not, however, be overlooked that Madison stoutly opposed another necessary decision of the Convention as to the equality of the voice of the States in the Senate. He said that the Convention "was reduced to the alternative of either departing from justice in order to conciliate the smaller States and the minority of the people of the United States, or of displeasing them by justly gratifying the larger States and the majority of the people. He could not himself hesitate as to the option he ought to make. . . . If the principal States comprehending a majority of the people of the United States should concur in a just and judicious plan, he had the firmest hopes that all the other States would by degrees accede to it." But by a close vote, Madison's position on this crucial question was disapproved, and the decision went in favor of the equal suffrage of the States in the Senate.

While Madison's paramount purpose was to rescue the people from the perils of an existing condition bordering on anarchy, and to maintain justice between the States, he was also intent upon preserving the rights of the States. In his view, it was through the Union that the States themselves were to be preserved. His conception was of the needs of a great people, and as he put it "the Federal and State Governments are in fact but different agents and trustees of the people, constituted with different powers, and designed for different purposes." Madison was seeking not to impair the necessary functions of state governments, but by conserving the essential interests of national security and stability to make it possible for the people in their respective States to enjoy the advantages of the peaceful administration of their local affairs.

Madison very clearly recognized the necessity of providing for invalidating state legislation which might be repugnant to the federal authority as granted by the Constitution. The Virginia Plan proposed to confer upon the national legislature the power "to negative all laws passed by the several States contravening in the opinion of the national legislature the Articles of Union." In describing the action of the Convention, Madison explained that "The obvious necessity of a control on the laws of the States, so far as they might violate the Constitution and laws of the United States, left no option but as to the mode. The modes presenting themselves were: (1) a veto of the passage of the State laws; (2) a Congressional repeal of them; (3) a Judicial annulment of them. The first, though extensively favored at the outset, was found, on discussion, liable to insuperable objections arising from the extent of country and the multiplicity of State laws. The second was not free from such as gave a preference to the *third* as now provided by the Constitution." And again, referring to what he termed the "supremacy of the Judicial power" in this respect, Madison said, in one of his latest writings: "I have never ceased to think that this supremacy was a vital principle of the Constitution as it is a prominent feature in its text. . . . I have never been able to see, that without such a view of the subject the Constitution itself could be the supreme law of the land; or that the *uniformity* of the Federal Authority throughout the parties to it could be preserved; or that without this *uniformity*, anarchy and disunion could be prevented." That was Madison's view of the essential function of the Supreme Court of the United States. It was very clearly expressed in a letter to Jefferson in 1823, when he sent to Jefferson a copy of his letters to Spencer Roane, a correspondence growing out of the decision in *Cohens* v. *Virginia*,[1] holding that the Supreme Court had jurisdiction on a writ of error to a state court in a state criminal prosecution. Madison had there said: "The Gordian Knot of the Constitution

[1] 6 Wheaton, 264.

seems to lie in the problem of collision between the federal and state powers, especially as eventually exercised by their respective tribunals. If the knot cannot be untied by the text of the Constitution it ought not, certainly, to be cut by any political Alexander."

Without attempting to review the history or content of the Virginia Resolutions of 1798, which Madison drafted, or the Kentucky Resolutions of the same year, it is sufficient for the present purpose to say that when South Carolina in 1832 passed its Nullification Ordinance, Madison disclaimed any intention in preparing the Virginia Resolutions to support what he called "the colossal heresy" of the nullifiers or to express disapproval of the jurisdiction of the Supreme Court in passing upon the validity of the legislation of the Congress. What he had in mind was a common protest by the States against federal legislation deemed to be in excess of the power of Congress. As he said in his Report on the Virginia Resolutions: "The declarations in such cases are expressions of opinion, unaccompanied with any other effect than what they may produce on opinion by exciting reflection. The expositions of the judiciary, on the other hand, are carried into immediate effect by force. The former may lead to a change in the legislative expression of the general will — possibly, to a change in the opinion of the judiciary, the latter enforces the general will, whilst that will and that opinion continue unchanged." Madison believed that "the nullifying claims if reduced to practice, instead of being the conservative principle of the Constitution, would necessarily, and it may be said obviously, be a deadly poison."

The Constitution as adopted by the Convention did not conform in all respects to Madison's views, still less to those of Hamilton. But both, yielding to a conviction of the paramount necessity of ratification, united in a collaboration of luminous reasoning and persuasive argument which has no parallel in political literature. The papers of the *Federalist* are an enduring monument to the intellectual power and patriotic zeal of both Hamilton and Madison. Whatever their later differences, in the cause of the ratification of the Constitution they worked as one. And there was need of their best efforts. While Madison observed that "the case in Virginia seems to prove that the body of sober and steady people, even of the lower order, are tired of the vicissitudes, injustices, and follies which have so much characterized public measures, and are impatient for some change which promises stability and repose," the opponents of ratification were formidable. In Virginia the situation was critical. "The General and Admiralty Courts, with most of the Bar," said Madison, "oppose the Constitution. . . . Mr. Henry is the great adversary who will render the event precarious." Madison thus had the opportunity of crowning his service in the Convention by his defense of its work. In the opposition along with Patrick Henry were found such antagonists as Richard Henry Lee, George Mason, James Monroe, and Benjamin Harrison. Madison had the advantage of precise and comprehensive knowledge of his subject. Beveridge gives us a striking picture of Madison's appearance as he rose to speak : "The chair recognized a slender, short-statured man of thirty-seven, wearing a handsome costume of blue and buff with doubled straight collar and white ruffles on breast and at wrists. His hair, combed forward to conceal baldness, was powdered and fell behind in the long beribboned queue of fashion. He was so small that he could not be seen by all the members ; and his voice was so weak that only rarely could he be heard throughout the hall. Such was James Madison as he stood, hat in hand and his notes in his hat, and began the first of those powerful speeches, the strength of which, in spite of poor reporting, has projected itself through more than a hundred years." With the decisive influence of Washington's support, the Constitution was ratified in the Convention by a slender majority. While New Hampshire's ratification had given the requisite nine State votes, failure in Virginia would probably have been followed by failure in New York, with most serious consequences.

Yet, even with that success, Madison's labors for our constitutional system were not ended. There was widespread dissatisfaction because of the absence of a Bill of Rights. Madison had not seen in the Constitution those serious dangers "which alarmed many respectable citizens," but he welcomed the opportunity to demonstrate anew his devotion to individual liberty. Accordingly, in the first Congress under the Constitution, he proposed the amendments which should satisfy "the public mind that their liberties will be perpetual." These had the provisions which are now found in substance in the first ten Amendments to the Constitution. In thus maintaining, as against interference by the Federal Government, the rights of freedom of conscience, of speech, and of the press, of trial by jury, and immunity from unreasonable searches and seizures, in providing the guaranty against deprivation of life, liberty, and property without due process of law, Madison had in mind protection against both Legislature and Executive, and for the maintenance of these guarantees he relied upon an independent Judiciary. "If," said he, in proposing the Amendments, "they are incorporated into the Constitution, independent tribunals will consider themselves in a peculiar manner the guardians of those rights; they will be an impenetrable bulwark against every assumption of power in the Legislative or Executive; they will be naturally led to resist every encroachment upon rights expressly stipulated for in the Constitution by the Declaration of Rights." Thus Madison who had insisted upon adequate national power operating directly upon the people, and that the new constitutional government must be "founded on the people" through ratification in State Conventions chosen in each State, justifying the inspiring words of the Preamble — "We the people of the United States" — evidenced his deepest conviction that the ultimate purpose of the Constitution was to maintain the security and the opportunity of the individual citizen.

Madison had read too widely and had thought too deeply to put his ultimate trust in any form of words, even if they were endowed with the solemnity of a Constitution and were formulated and approved with the utmost deliberation. Political wisdom might erect the structure, but the result would depend upon the use that was made of it. Madison had no illusions as to the source of the dangers to the interests he had sought so earnestly to safeguard. Power could always be abused. "Wherever the real power in a government lies," he remarked in a letter to Jefferson in 1788, "there is the danger of oppression. In our governments the real power lies in the majority of the community, and the invasion of private rights is *chiefly* to be apprehended, not from acts of government contrary to the sense of its constituents, but from acts in which the government is the mere instrument of the major number of the constituents. . . . Wherever there is an interest and power to do wrong, wrong will generally be done, and not less readily by a powerful and interested party than by a powerful and interested prince."

In his preparation of the Great Convention, Madison had voiced the perennial complaint of the multiplicity of laws. His comment upon this evil of his own time is not without an amusing aspect in the light of the conditions of our day. Said he, "As far as laws are necessary to mark with precision the duties of those who are to obey them, and to take from those who are to administer them a discretion which might be abused, their number is the price of liberty. As far as laws exceed this limit, they are a nuisance; a nuisance of the most pestilent kind. Try the codes of the several States by this test, and what a luxuriancy of legislation do they present. The short period of independency has filled as many pages as the century which preceded it. Every year, almost every session, adds a new volume!" But it was the injustice of the laws as he found them that gave him the greater anxiety. As he put it, "If the multiplicity and mutability of laws prove a want of wisdom, their injustice betrays a defect still more alarming; more alarming not merely because it is a greater evil in itself; but because it brings more into question the fundamental principle of republican government that the majority who rule in such governments are the safest guardians both of public good and private rights." And "the great desideratum in government" he thought to be "such a modification of the sovereignty as will render it sufficiently neutral between the different interests and factions, to control one part of the society from invading the rights of another, and at the same time sufficiently controlled itself, from setting up an interest adverse to that of the whole society."

The problem of securing a just and efficient government is far more difficult today than when Madison made these observations. It is the irony of the present situation, that in the hour of the apparent triumph of democracy, when the rule of peoples instead of monarchs was thought to have been made secure, there should be the most serious challenge of democratic ideals. The challenge is more fundamental than one to the particular forms of democratic or republican institutions. It is a challenge to the efficiency, wisdom, and justice of popular rule carried on through the instrumentalities of responsible legislators and administrators. Whether the attack is in the interest of the State conceived as the protector of the social interests of all the people, or it is motivated by class consciousness in a particular interest, there is common ground in denying the capacity of the people to make laws and to execute them through representatives freely chosen without dictatorship. For the delays and ineptitude of parliaments it is sought to substitute the promptitude and vigor of executive power, and self-constituted authorities assume the responsibility of supplying the intelligence which government by the people is said to lack.

The challenge is not simply to the democratic principle with respect to the source of authority in government, but to the ideals of liberty. For the alternative to democratic institutions is found in despotic power, whether or not exercised with benevolent intent. The final questions are the extent to which governmental coercion is to be permitted to proceed and who is to be allowed to exert it. It was the ideal of the fathers that our government should be representative and responsible ; that our institutions should provide unity and stability, with the limitation of national power to appropriate national ends and with the circumscribing of both federal and state authority in order that a fair freedom of individual opportunity might be preserved. There is no indication that we desire to abandon this system in favor of any form of autocracy, whether contrived to promote efficiency or to establish class rule. With all the imperfections of our institutions we have not yielded to despair. We desire to foster our collective interests, but we have not yet been persuaded that we should be the gainers in the end either by subordinating all individual concerns to the wholly uncontrolled will of the majority or by submitting to any sort of dictatorship.

We cannot fail to realize, however, that our governmental system is most complex. It makes extraordinary demands upon intelligent political activity and upon capacity for self-restraint. We cannot save ourselves by worshiping the forms of our institutions if we fail to make them serve our just interests. Success in solving our problems lies in a wise application of Madison's controlling principle of the maintenance of a strong national government together with the essential authority of the States over their local affairs, and with constant respect for those individual rights which experience and conscience teach us should be inviolable. It was preëminently the political genius of Madison which has given us opportunity, and we shall profit in our use of it to the extent that we emulate his example in making reason, and not emotion, our guide. We need leadership in thought even more than leadership in action. And to James Madison who gave that leadership, when it was needed most, we render our homage.

JAMES MONROE

President of the United States

1817–1825

The Honorable ANDREW JACKSON MONTAGUE, *The Speaker*

FROM THE INTRODUCTION OF THE SPEAKER
by
GOVERNOR POLLARD

In these notable ceremonies in honor of our eight Virginia born Presidents we have now come to the unveiling of the bust of James Monroe. This bust, which is made after the famous original by Houdon, the great artist brought from France by Virginia to model the likeness of George Washington, is the work of the distinguished sculptor, Mr. Attilio Piccirilli, formerly of Italy and now of New York, a sculptor famed for his works of art on two continents. The donor of the bust is Mr. Jay Winston Johns, a Pittsburg-Virginian. Mr. Johns is the owner and restorer of Ash Lawn, the picturesque home of James Monroe, and is a man who knows and loves Virginia. To him for his restoration of Monroe's home and his presentation of this bust, Virginia owes a debt of lasting gratitude.

* *

Many times have I congratulated myself on having been able to secure as speakers for these occasions men whose peculiar fitness for the task is at once recognized. The address on George Wash-

ATTILIO PICCIRILLI, *The Sculptor*

ington was delivered by Dr. Albert Bushnell Hart, a noted historian. Thomas Jefferson was interpreted by the Honorable John W. Davis, who now carries on the Jefferson ideals. James Madison was represented by Chief Justice Charles Evans Hughes, who presides over the Supreme Court of the United States, which Madison helped to create. We are especially fortunate in the speaker for this occasion. Those acquainted with the careers of James Monroe and of Andrew Jackson Montague will not need to ask why Andrew Jackson Montague was chosen to interpret the

JAY WINSTON JOHNS, *The Donor*

career and achievements of President Monroe.   Both were Governors
of Virginia, both were members of the Congress of the United States,
and both were profound students of international affairs, and each
has adorned with culture and patriotism the respective generations
in which he lived.

JAMES MONROE

ADDRESS BY

The Honorable ANDREW J. MONTAGUE

Y our Excellency, Ladies, and Gentlemen :
James Monroe was born in Westmoreland County,
Virginia, in a few miles of the birthplace of Washington,
on April 28, 1758. He was born of goodly stock, in a
goodly place, and at a goodly time. His first Westmoreland ancestor was a sea captain, as was John Washington,
the father of George. His father, Spence Monroe, was of
Scotch descent, and his mother, Elizabeth Jones, of Welsh.
Her brother, Joseph Jones, of King George County, was a
man of great ability, an eminent jurist, and an influential
statesman. He was devoted to his nephew, James, and did
much to encourage and direct the course of his early life.
Monroe's father was a farmer, inheriting and purchasing
large tracts of land, discharging with efficiency and fidelity
several local public offices, and a signer of the famous
Westmoreland Resolutions in relation to the British Stamp
Act. James was a boy of nine at this time, and with a
natural aptitude for politics, he must have been impressed
by this event.

His birthplace was in an extraordinary environment of
nourishing associations and influences. In a radius of
fifty miles from his home were living the great thinkers and
founders of American free institutions. He was almost in

sound of the voices of Washington, Madison, Marshall, George Mason, and the Lees. Substantially within this radius lived Patrick Henry and Samuel Davies, later the first great President of Princeton, Pendleton and Taylor of Caroline, Francis Corbin of Middlesex, Carter Braxton of King and Queen, and John Rodgers Clarke of Orange. Thomas Jefferson was near by, and, though fifteen years older, was his devoted and cherished friend. What commanding contacts! What ennobling and instructive associations! This environment was in itself a subconscious education that ultimately swept him far upon the ocean of fame.

In the narrow sense, his education was limited, as it was of most of the famous men of that day. There were no great school buildings, but there were a few great teachers. Among these was the Rev. William Douglas, probably brought from Scotland by the Monroe family. He taught Thomas Jefferson for four years, and also for a while Monroe. The Henry family secured Thomas Campbell, the poet, but he was compelled to forego his journey to Virginia, and in his stead came Archibald Campbell, his uncle, a fine teacher. Madison attended this school, and it is said that Washington and the elder Marshall did — certain it is that Monroe and John Marshall were here together for two years — here began their lifelong friendship, here they were well grounded in Latin and mathematics, and prepared for college.

What college should Monroe attend? Out of about one hundred and twenty boys who had gone from Virginia to English universities up to this period nineteen came from Westmoreland. But Monroe and his family were intensely Virginians, and naturally he was entered in the College of William and Mary, then the richest college in America and entering upon its golden opportunity, as Williamsburg had now become the new capital of Virginia. The Capitol itself was an attractive building, situated at one end of the Duke of Gloucester Street, and the College, the architectural creation of Sir Christopher Wrenn, stood at the other, in full view each of the other.

Monroe was now a well-grown young man. Tall, square shouldered, sinewy, active, and energetic, with a grave face, steady, kindly, penetrating bluish gray eyes, modest but unafraid. He entered college in the fall of 1774, and he was now in another but invigorating community. He had left the land of the Washingtons and the Lees; he was now in the land of Pocahontas and John Smith, of Wythe, the Randolphs, Tylers, Tuckers, Blairs, Harrisons, and Roane. Here the cultured president and faculty of the College became his immediate and dominating influence. Nor did he lose sight of the House of Burgesses and its political activities, with its varied membership. Bruton Church, with its beauty, dignity, and spiritual appeal, deeply impressed him. Nor was he unmindful of the glamour of the Royal Governor and his court. Raleigh Tavern was then kept by Anthony Hay, whose son George was to become in due time United States Attorney, the official prosecutor of Aaron Burr for treason, United States District Judge, and the husband of Eliza, the daughter of Monroe.

The College had not more than seventy matriculates at this time, among whom were three sons of Dunmore and some others who grew to deserved distinction in field and forum and council. Of course, a boy with Monroe's political aptitudes knew all of his classmates! College records give an inadequate picture of the life and activities of students. The bursar's books contain Monroe's expenditures for matriculation and board and keep. There remains, however, a paper in the form of a petition, with

Monroe among the signers, protesting against the extravagance and partiality of Mistress Digges, the matron; but upon its hearing by the Board, Monroe admitted he signed without reading the paper, an age-old ending of this common and futile procedure. He was a diligent and faithful student, and the training here acquired soon reflected itself in a long, varied, and illustrious public career.

Monroe's college education came to an end in the second year of his matriculation. Rumblings of revolution could be heard from Massachusetts to Georgia, and the great men whom I have heretofore mentioned were especially responsive to the multiplied signs of the time. Patrick Henry's dramatic utterance "that after all we must fight" was caught up and repeated by the students throughout the college. The Resolution of the Virginia Convention instructing her delegates in the Continental Congress to propose a Declaration of Independence, and the oppressive acts of Parliament and King were rapidly culminating in this portentous event, which in turn would culminate in a mighty epoch. So Monroe was born at a goodly time.

Monroe's college books were laid aside. Some two hundred Virginia troops quaintly uniformed "in green hunting shirts, homespun, homewoven and homemade, with the words of 'Liberty or Death' in large white letters on their bosoms" appeared upon the campus, the greens, and the streets of Williamsburg. Monroe was deeply impressed by these troops, for among them was Lieutenant John Marshall, his friend and fellow student under Parson Campbell. These were the "minute men" of Culpeper, Fauquier, and Orange. Several of the students of the college rode great distances carrying messages in relation to the impending struggle. Grigsby alludes to "two tall and gallant youths," Monroe and Marshall, about to become officers under General Washington. Marshall became a member of the eleventh, and Monroe of the third Virginia Regiments. Monroe was also of the small company who moved the arms from the palace to the powder house in Williamsburg, and a little later he was in active service in the far north. He participated in the battle of Harlem Heights, his company being commanded by Captain Washington, a kinsman of the great General. Monroe was greatly relied upon by his superior officers.

He was with his military unit at White Plains and at Trenton. In the battle of Trenton the advance guard of the American troops was led by Captain William Washington and Lieutenant James Monroe, repulsing the British and capturing two pieces of artillery in a fierce engagement. Captain Washington received a shot in the wrist, and Lieutenant Monroe one through the shoulder, carrying the bullet to his grave. It is believed he crossed the Delaware with George Washington; at any rate, he was among the first and foremost at Trenton.

Monroe's efficiency and gallantry was recognized by General Washington himself, who said: "The zeal he discovered by entering the service at an early period, the character he supported in his regiment, and the manner in which he distinguished himself at Trenton, when he received a wound, induced me to appoint him to a captaincy in one of the additional regiments. This regiment failing, from the difficulty of recruiting, he entered into Lord Stirling's family and has served two campaigns as a volunteer aid to his lordship. He has in every instance maintained the reputation of a brave, active, and sensible officer."

Later he served as an aide with the rank of Major on the staff of Lord Stirling, and took part in the battles of Brandywine, Germantown, and Monmouth. He was subsequently made Lieutenant Colonel before he was twenty-one, and displayed great energy and ability as commissioner to investigate and report upon the condition of the southern army, when his military career ended.

Monroe now determined to make his way in civil life, and adopted the legal profession as his calling. He studied law under Thomas Jefferson, which association increased the confidence and affection of each in the other. The political activities of Monroe were now so multiplied that he pursued his practice with many interruptions, but he was a lawyer of learning and ability, as is shown by his selection as one of the famous commission appointed to revise the laws of the new State.

He was early chosen as a Delegate to the General Assembly from King George County. He became also a member of the Executive Council, and was elected to the fourth, fifth, and sixth Congresses of the Confederation. For a second time he was returned to the General Assembly, and later became a member of the "great convention" of Virginia that considered the adoption of the Federal Constitution.

His Congressional experience under the Articles of Confederation had inclined him to a stronger Federal union. A government that could tax but could not collect was an anomaly. In this Congress Monroe became deeply interested in three subjects: the great back or western country; the Mississippi, its navigation and an outlet at New Orleans to the sea (this was the germ and genesis of the Louisiana Purchase); and the regulation of commerce, the matrix of the new Federal Constitution. He drew the famous report in this Congress upon this subject, and its expressions and implications are to the effect that this regulation requires a stronger government. Bancroft thinks Monroe failed to give to this measure which he

[94]

proposed his full support. The evidence fails to sustain this prejudiced conclusion. No one would have been more critical of this position if true than Jefferson, yet he was warmly then Monroe's friend.

He had favored a new Constitution, but in the Virginia Convention he aligned himself with Henry, Mason, and Lee against its ratification and against Washington, Madison, and Marshall. Why this change of front? It required independence and courage to do it. But he lacked neither. He was a man of strong convictions. But now the man of the hour was Madison. Bancroft declares that in this time of despair "the country was lifted by Madison and Virginia." "We now come," says he, "upon the week glorious for Virginia beyond any event in its annals, or in the history of any republic that had ever before existed." Virginia evoked and secured the new Federal Convention at Philadelphia, which Monroe approved, for he was fundamentally a Union man, though he did not approve all of its powers. He made two speeches in the Virginia Convention. He thought the consolidation powers too great; there was no Bill of Rights; the President should hold office for one term of seven years; and the eastern States might block the development of the central and western sections of the country. He would support the Constitution with amendments but not without them. Hugh Blair Grigsby writes that: "The speech of Monroe was well received. It made upon the House a strong impression, which was heightened by the modesty of his demeanor, by the sincerity which was reflected from every feature of his honest face, and by the minute knowledge which he exhibited of a historical transaction of surpassing interest to the South." Henry, the greatest of American orators, followed and rose to surpassing heights. Associating himself with a storm that broke

[95]

upon the building he climaxed the scene with such transcendent oratory that "the members rose in confusion, and the meeting was dissolved." But Washington and Madison won; and in later years the Republic faced a catastrophe that of itself lent much support to Monroe's fears and prophesies. He accepted patriotically the result of the Convention, and labored in and out of season to make the new Federal Charter operative and successful.

Notwithstanding his objections to the Constitution, which were soon substantially removed by amendments as the result of the fight made by Henry, Mason, and himself, he became a candidate for the first Congress, and by the irony of fate his opponent was his friend, James Madison. He should not have opposed Madison, but no doubt he became a candidate by reason of the persistence of Henry and other friends of the Virginia Convention. It was a unique and picturesque campaign, resulting in Monroe's defeat by a majority of three hundred.

But the new Congress was soon to find him in its higher branch. Virginia's first Senators were Richard Henry Lee and William Grayson, a near kinsman of Monroe, and who with Lee had also opposed the new Federal Constitution. Grayson lived but a short while and Monroe was elected by the General Assembly to the vacancy, taking his seat in December, 1790, at the age of thirty-two, and serving until May, 1794. Thus Monroe was again in close touch with his friend Thomas Jefferson, who was then at the seat of government in Philadelphia as Secretary of State in Washington's Cabinet.

Monroe was a hard-working Senator. He spoke infrequently, but practically and rigidly to the point. His committee assignments were good, and he was most industrious in performing his duties. He was pronounced in his opinions, which in a political sense tended to the

liberalism of the school of Jefferson. Gouverneur Morris'
confirmation as Minister to France, and Jay's to England,
were opposed by Monroe. He thought Jay's position as
to the Mississippi radically wrong.

Monroe now looked forward to a long Senatorial
career. He purchased a home in Albemarle County near
Monticello, and worked upon the revision of laws of
Virginia. But suddenly the stage of his activities shifted.
He was taken from the Senate so to speak, and to his great
surprise nominated by the President and quickly confirmed
as Minister to France. He arrived in Paris on August 2,
1794, but was not officially received until August 15. The
French Revolution was rolling along in its bloody way;
Robespierre expired under the ax of his Brutus, and
organized government for appropriate reception of foreign diplomats was nebulous. The Committee of Public
Safety hesitated to receive him. He took the bull by
the horns after ten days waiting and addressed the President and Representatives of the Convention, stating
that he did not know the "competent department nor
the forms established by law for his reception." A de-
cree was at once passed inviting him to the bosom of the
Convention. He promptly accepted, making his address
in English, with a translation in French, that was read by
the Secretary, together with two letters from Edmund
Randolph, the American Secretary of State. The speech
was dignified and glowing in style. It made a profound
impression, and was printed by order of "the Convention,
in two languages, French and American." He was enthusiastically received, the President giving him the fraternal
embrace or *accolade*. The whole ceremony was novel and
dramatic. Monroe was then most cordially welcomed by
officials and citizens, and the success of his mission seemed
assured. But diplomacy is a fickle jade, and ambushes lay

on every side. Jay was at St. James. He had negotiated a treaty with England which was very offensive to the French, to a majority of the American people, and to Monroe. America was practically facing war with both nations, and Jay's treaty threw America into the arms of Great Britain and into the face of France. Monroe's government had not apprised him of the text or contents of this treaty until it reached the public. He was justly indignant at this, for he had no opportunity to parry or soften its effect upon the French. Then too, Randolph thought Monroe was too glowing in his address, that he had gone beyond the scope of his agency, and severely criticized his conduct. Monroe was recalled by Pickering, Randolph's successor, on August 22, thus serving at the French post only thirteen days, but he did not take his leave until December 30. He was very indignant. He avouched his letter of instructions from Randolph, submitting his actions to be fully within the scope of his instructions. And they clearly were. But really Monroe was in no way to blame. There was nothing that he did or failed to do that was incompatible with his instructions or his mission. Under the guise of neutrality our government preferred Great Britain, although it had previously preferred France under the treaty of 1778. A government which practices neutrality should be most rigid in applying the same treatment to all nations. The Secretary had bungled and Monroe had to suffer. Monroe returned to Virginia, and wrote a lengthy defense of some five hundred pages. It is an interesting and able document, and vindicated him at home, for he was elected Governor of Virginia in 1799, and twice reëlected, holding office until 1802. He was again elected in 1811, but resigned to enter the Cabinet of Madison.

Within the limitations of time no adequate discussion

can be made of his conduct as Governor of Virginia.
Monroe was very thorough, painstaking, a master of
details, courageous, and just-minded. He was tempera-
mentally an administrator. He acted with energy, decision, and humaneness in his first administration in an
uprising of some thousand or more negroes led by two
slaves, "General Gabriel" and "Jack Bowler," for the
destruction of Richmond.

Jefferson, the Secretary of State, had no hazy ideas about
New Orleans. He knew its possession by the United
States was essential to their safety and development, and he
was alarmed at its retrocession by Spain to France. The
former nation was a languid owner, and we could live side
by side with her without difficulty for some time to come.
Not so with France. Jefferson said : "The day that France
takes possession of New Orleans fixes the sentence which
is to retain her forever within the low-water mark. It
seals the union of two nations who, in conjunction, can
maintain exclusive possession of the ocean. From that
moment we must marry ourselves to the British fleet and
nation." The letter containing these graphic observations
was sent to Livingston, our Minister at Paris, by du Pont
Nemours, who was requested to see Napoleon unofficially,
and impress upon him "the idea that if he should occupy
Louisiana, the United States would wait a few years until
the next war between France and England, but would then
make common cause with England."

Livingston made slow headway in acquiring New
Orleans. He wrote Madison on January 13, 1802, that
there "was no government where less could be done by
negotiations than France." "There are," said he, "no
people, no legislature, no counselors. One man is every-
thing. . . . He seldom asks advice and never hears it
unasked. His ministers are mere clerks, and his legislature

and counselors parade officers." A graphic picture of Bonaparte is this. Jefferson and Livingston did not fully agree, the latter holding the opinion that "so long as France conforms to existing treaties" between the United States and Spain it would be unwise to oppose the transfer of this territory to France. So Jefferson needed some one in France other than Livingston, and Monroe was that man. His nomination as Envoy Extraordinary to France was sent to the Senate on January 10, 1803. He was quickly confirmed, and lost no time in sailing, which he did upon a ship of four hundred tons, named *Richmond*.

Parenthetically it is interesting to observe that almost at this precise time Jefferson recommended Lewis and Clarke for the exploration of the upper Mississippi River and the northwestern country.

Livingston wished the assistance of Monroe, to whom he wrote a welcoming letter upon his arrival at Havre on April 10, 1803. "I congratulate you," said Livingston, "upon your safe arrival. We have long and anxiously waited for you. God grant that your mission may answer your and the public expectation. War may do something for us; nothing else would. I have paved the way for you, and if you could add to my memoirs an assurance that we were now in the possession of New Orleans, we should do well."

The evidence shows that on this very day, April 10, Easter Sunday, Bonaparte discussed New Orleans with Talleyrand and Marbois. They were divided in opinion, and the conference was carried far into the night, the ministers remaining at St. Cloud. About daybreak Bonaparte, having received alarming dispatches from England, summoned Marbois, and said; "I renounce Louisiana. Negotiate for its cession. Don't wait for Monroe. I want fifty million francs; for less I will not treat. Acquaint me day by day, hour by hour, with your progress. Keep Talleyrand informed." New Orleans was embraced in the larger cession. Bonaparte needed money for his war; so he and he alone initiated the larger transaction. Livingston did not do it; Monroe did not do it; Bonaparte did it. When he wished to do a thing he had no illusions and no scruples. Marbois told Livingston of Bonaparte's offer, and Livingston at once undertook to anticipate and exclude Monroe in the negotiations and latterly contended that Monroe had nothing to do with the transaction. Livingston and the United States were after New Orleans, whereas Bonaparte surprised the envoys by offering to sell the whole of Louisiana. This territory was then offered to the United States for one hundred million francs and the payment of the claims of American nationals.

Livingston pronounced the consideration exorbitant, he could reach no conclusion without consulting Monroe; but Livingston sat up until three o'clock at night writing a dispatch to Madison apprising him of the interview with Marbois, and declaring that the purchase was wise. Livingston also made the astounding suggestion that if the price was too high, the outlay might be reimbursed by the "sale of territory west of the Mississippi, with the right of sovereignty to some power in Europe, whose vicinity we should not fear." Livingston and Monroe then agreed to give fifty million francs, but in the spirit of trade offered forty million, one-half to be returned to American claimants. Marbois regretted that we could not give more, and declared that he must consult the Consul before he could accept. Latterly Marbois proposed eighty million francs, and our envoys at last acceded to his figures. Thus ended the largest real estate transaction that the world has ever known, which was conducted by

Bonaparte with as much nonchalance as if the property was a small town lot. He remarked exultingly to the Envoys, "I have given to England a maritime rival that will sooner or later humble her pride"; and upon taking leave of Monroe on June 24, he declared "that the cession he had made was not so much on account of the price given as for the motives of policy; and that he wished for friendship between the Republics." This great man was not very veracious.

✗ The development of our country is closely connected with this famous purchase. Without it perhaps there would have been no Missouri Compromise, no annexation of Texas, no Northwestern Territory, no acquisition of Northern Mexico or California, no Nebraska Bill, no Indian troubles, no Alaskan Purchase, no Pacific railroads, no isthmus canal, no Chinese immigration, perhaps no war between the States, for it is difficult to affirm that any of these controversies or events would have ever been known if Spain, France, or Great Britain had remained in possession of the domain beyond the Mississippi.

Our government wished to acquire Florida, and Monroe was especially charged to undertake this negotiation with Spain. This duty did not devolve upon Livingston, but we find him trying to anticipate and perhaps supplant Monroe in this negotiation, which conduct throws light upon similar action of Livingston in the Louisiana negotiations. Spain, however, was unwilling to consider the question, which was postponed to the administration of Monroe. No criticism should attach to Monroe. He displayed great tact, industry, and sagacity in the negotiations.

Monroe was not only a special envoy to France but to England and Spain as well. Pinkney of Maryland was sent over to assist him in negotiating a treaty with England. After arduous and tactful efforts, and delays by reason of changes and deaths in the English ministry, a treaty was signed. But the exasperating subject of impressment of American seamen, and compensation for loss of American property, was not embraced in the document, and Jefferson never transmitted it to the Senate. Monroe and Pinkney were disappointed, for they wished to avoid war, and the former wrote the Secretary of State a full explanation of his conduct.

Monroe had returned home, and was again and for the fourth time elected Governor of Virginia, a very extraordinary expression of the confidence and esteem of those who knew him best.

England and America were now drifting rapidly into collision. The British naval vessel *Leopard*, asserting the right of search, had wantonly attacked the American frigate *Chesapeake* off the Virginia capes, again delaying action upon the treaty, which, however, was abruptly abandoned when the odious and menacing "Orders in Council" were issued by England, thereby rendering inevitable war between the two nations. Perceval's truculent declaration in February, 1812, that England could not listen to the pretensions of neutral nations caused Russell, the American Minister at London, to write home that war could not honorably be avoided. Madison, now President, had exhausted all honorable means to do so, and Monroe, now the new Secretary of State, had long been indefatigable to this end. War was declared on June 18, 1812, the message submitting the question to Congress, as well as the report from the committee headed by the renowned Calhoun, were written by Monroe himself, Henry Adams to the contrary notwithstanding.

The war opened brilliantly for America on lake and sea, and was likewise conducted from Canada to New

Orleans with the humiliating exceptions of Bladensburg and Washington, which were captured and subjected to barbaric usages, to burning without justification both the White House and the Capitol. This invasion roused the pacific Madison, who now threw himself upon the strong arm of Monroe, who was at once made Secretary of War in addition to the portfolio of State which he was filling with efficiency and distinction. Monroe quickly infused vigor, energy, and optimism in the army. It may, in passing, be of interest to observe that Monroe's service as Secretary of State was interrupted by four several assignments to perform the duties of Secretary of War. He, as before suggested, endeavored to secure treaties of peace with England; but failing, he saw war as the inexorable and honorable fate, and he did not hesitate so to declare. It should here be said that Monroe's whole conduct in relation to the war was patriotic in conception, and wise and daring in execution. His courage, his self-control, his patience, his incomparable experience, his energy, and his profound and penetrating mind made him more effective than "an army with banners." He was now indeed Madison's right arm!

The war over, the treaty of Ghent ratified, and the Federalist party dissolving, partisan rancors subsiding, and the dissensions of sections disappearing, Madison, the political philosopher and patriot, realized the triumph of his administration, and was content to trust its justification to posterity.

But time was now approaching for the choice of his successor. Governor Sullivan, of Massachusetts, declared that the Virginians had held the Presidency "as often as they were entitled to," and therefore advocated the election of DeWitt Clinton as the successor of Madison. Monroe was nominated in a caucus of the Republican or Democratic members of Congress over William H. Crawford, of Georgia, by a vote of 65 to 54, and in the Electoral College with a total vote of 221 Monroe received 183 as against 34 for Rufus King. He was inaugurated March 4, 1817, amidst Senators, Representatives, Galliard, the President of the Senate, and Henry Clay, the Speaker of the House, foreign ministers, Justices of the Supreme Court, including the illustrious Chief Justice Marshall, who administered the oath of office to the new President. Boys at Campbell's school, now standing face to face on the same platform, had become the two greatest living figures in the world.

What an incomparable career was Monroe's! Lieutenant in the Continental Army, and Lieutenant Colonel before he was twenty-one; Military Commissioner to the Southern Army; Member of the General Assembly of Virginia; Member of the Executive Council; Member of the Continental Congress; Member again of the General Assembly; Member of the Virginia Convention to ratify the Federal Constitution; United States Senator; Member of Commission for revising the laws of Virginia; twice Minister to France; four times Governor of Virginia; Minister to England and Spain; signer of the treaty acquiring Louisiana; third time Member of the General Assembly of Virginia; Secretary of State; Secretary of War; twice President of the United States; author of the Monroe Doctrine; Visitor of the University of Virginia; Member and President of the Virginia Constitutional Convention of 1829–30; and Justice of the Peace.

> *"Thou hast it now, King, Cawdor, Glamis, all,*
> *"As the weird woman promised."*

I will pass briefly to consider him as the fifth President of the United States. Twice was he President, and the

[105]

second time elected with but one dissenting vote. This was the "era of good feeling." He was a successful and able Chief Magistrate; impeccably honorable, and self-sacrificingly patriotic. The Federalist party disappeared under his administration, and he received substantially the united support of his countrymen. But I can only consider one of his many administrative achievements, and that is America's greatest foreign policy, for which his name is the synonym — "The Monroe Doctrine."

Was Rush, Adams, Canning, Jefferson, Madison, or Monroe the author of this doctrine? The evidence of record is perfectly clear that Monroe himself and no one else was its author. He wrote it, signed it, and sent it to Congress. No other is responsible for it. It was Monroe's Doctrine, and since its promulgation it has borne no other name than his. Envy, jealousy, prejudice, and ignorance have alone sought to impair Monroe's authorship of this contribution to American politics. Of course he sought information and advice from informed and responsible statesmen. Why not? But does this absolve him from the responsibility and authorship of the paper?

Upon the fall of Napoleon, who had upset several of the European monarchies, a so-called Holy Alliance was instituted by Alexander I of Russia, and signed by Francis of Austria, Frederick William of Prussia, and Louis XVIII of France. The alliance was neither Holy nor Roman. It was a euphemistic title to conceal intrigues and to restore and extend European monarchies. One conspicuous design was to smother the fires in those South American countries that had been kindled by Miranda, Bolivar, and San Martin, and therein lurked the danger to the free institutions of the United States. Monroe sensed this. Canning suggested joint action by Great Britain and the United States to meet this unholy design. Monroe did not accept this offer, declaring that what should be done must be done by the United States alone of or for itself.

Monroe sent his message to Congress containing this doctrine on December, 1823, just as the expediency of sending ministers to the Congress of Panama was being debated. Adopting the digest made by Mr. Clark, sometime Under Secretary of State, the message substantially declares, —

1. The "American Continents," that is, North as well as South America, were not subject to colonization *by any European* power. This was concretely aimed at Russia, who was about to initiate such an undertaking in the far northwest of the United States.

2. The United States would consider any attempt of the "allied powers" to extend their system to any part of "this hemisphere as dangerous to our peace and safety."

3. "With existing colonies or dependencies of any European powers we have not interfered and shall not interfere."

4. With respect to Spanish Colonies which had declared and maintained their independence and which we had recognized, the United States "could not view any interposition for the purpose of oppressing them or of controlling in any other manner their destiny by any European power, in any other light than as the manifestation of an unfriendly disposition towards the United States."

5. The United States declared that it was impossible for these powers to extend their political system to North or South America "without endangering our peace and happiness," and that such interposition could not be considered with indifference.

6. The true policy was to leave Spain and her seceded colonies to adjust their differences between themselves. Thus the declaration falls into two divisions: future

colonization by any European power of the American continent; and "interposition for the purpose of oppressing them or of controlling in any other manner their destiny." The inhibitions apply to European powers, not to those of South or North America. The doctrine in origin and application is wholly one of self-preservation. The foothold of such powers upon this continent inevitably meant aggression upon the United States. This is practically the beginning and end of the doctrine that has become the fixed policy of our government which no informed and responsible American statesman will disregard.

James Monroe, while a member of the Continental Congress sitting in New York, married Elizabeth Kortright of that city in February, 1786. She was the daughter of Laurence Kortright, well known and well connected, and a lady of intelligence and culture. From a miniature of her painted in Paris, which Monroe thought her best likeness, she was of extraordinary beauty, which together with her tact and charm made her perhaps the most attractive chatelaine who ever lived in the White House, not excepting Dolly Madison. Several competent men and women who met them both were more attracted by Mrs. Monroe. Of this marriage there were two daughters, Eliza and Maria Hester, the former married George Hay, of whom I have heretofore spoken, and the latter, Samuel Gouverneur of New York, and some of the descendants of these daughters lend their presence to this occasion. Eliza went to school to the famous Madame Campan, and became a schoolmate of Hortense de Beauharnais, the daughter of Josephine, who married Louis Bonaparte, and became the mother of Napoleon III. She presented her own miniature to Eliza, together with a lock of her hair.

It was at the home of his daughter Maria, in New York, that Monroe died on July 4, 1831, at the age of seventy-three, his remains resting in that city until July 4, 1858, when they were removed with impressive ceremony and reinterred in our own Hollywood. The remains of his wife, who died at Oak Hill in Loudoun County some few years before his death, rest beside his tomb. Three Presidents of the United States died on the fourth of July, — Jefferson, Adams, and Monroe, the two former dying in the same year, 1826.

Monroe has not had full justice done him. He was malignantly criticized by his political partisans, and these criticisms have been magnified by some later writers.

He was an exemplary character. Jefferson affirmed that if his soul could be turned wrong side out, you would not find a speck upon it. His honor and courage and patriotism equaled that of any of our Presidents. He was also a man of great abilities. John Quincy Adams, his Secretary of State and subsequent President, entertained for his ability and character the greatest admiration. Calhoun thought his intellect of extraordinary power and penetration, declaring his capacity to consider a given subject, stripped of all irrelevant issues, and detached from all personal bias, to be equal to that of any man he ever knew. Lord Holland, in speaking of Monroe and his colleague Pinkney, whom he met in the negotiations about the English difficulties, declares that Monroe "had candor and principle"; that he was "diligent, earnest, sensible, and even a profound man"; and that while Pinkney was more attractive and brilliant his "opinions were neither so firmly rooted nor so deeply considered as those of Monroe."

Trevelyan in his *The American Revolution*, declares that "the junior officer in William Washington's company was a lad even younger than Hamilton, and not his equal (as indeed very few were) in intellectual endowments or in personal charm. And yet," said he, "if in the course of ages both their memories were to perish, that of Lieutenant Monroe would in all likelihood be the last forgotten of the two; for he was the James Monroe who in December, 1823, as the fifth President of the United States, enunciated the policy which defeated the machinations of the Holy Alliance, and which deprived Spain of her American colonies.''

Thus great achievements and their makers live and endure.

WILLIAM HENRY HARRISON

President of the United States

March 4 to April 4, 1841

Major-General CHARLES P. SUMMERALL, The Speaker

FROM THE INTRODUCTION OF THE SPEAKER

by

GOVERNOR POLLARD

American people honor in peace those who have served them in war. Presidents Washington, Jackson, William Henry Harrison, Taylor, Grant, and Benjamin Harrison are all conspicuous illustrations.

The Harrison family is unique in the history of this country. It furnished Benjamin Harrison, signer of the Declaration of Independence, his son William Henry Harrison, whom we honor today, and the grandson of the latter, Benjamin Harrison, President of the United States from 1889 to 1893.

William Henry Harrison because of his untimely death was President for only one month. His fame rests chiefly on his military career. It is, therefore, most fitting that the life of this great soldier of the last century should be interpreted for us by a great soldier of the present century.

The speaker of this occasion has been decorated by his own country for gallantry and for meritorious and distinguished service

CHESTER BEACH, *The Sculptor*

on the field of battle. Many other nations of the world have officially recognized his military genius. He stands out as one of the great figures of the World War. Nothing that can be said on this occasion will add to his distinction, but it may not be out of place to express the hope that the eventualities of history may add luster to his name by its coming to pass that the great struggle in which he was so conspicuously engaged shall prove in fact to be what it was in prophecy, "a war to end war."

Some of the great soldiers of history when the din of battle died from their ears have sunk back into lives of ease and disdained to

WILLIAM STEELE GRAY III, DAVID DUNLOP GRAY,
JOHN STUART GRAY, The Donors

take further part in the service of their country. Not so with
General Summerall. Like our own Robert E. Lee of the last
generation, and our own General Lejeune of this, he has given the
prestige of his name and the strength of his service to the education
of youth by accepting the Presidency of one of our most ancient and
honorable Southern institutions of learning. He thus becomes a
leader in peace as he was in war. Such a man, it is a pleasure to
see and hear.

*
* *

The bust of Harrison is the work of Chester Beach and is donated
by the children of Mrs. William S. Gray.

[115]

WILLIAM HENRY HARRISON

ADDRESS BY

Major-General CHARLES P. SUMMERALL

For the third time the City of Richmond is the scene of signal tribute to the services and fame of William Henry Harrison. The honor which the Commonwealth of Virginia has accorded today to the memory of one of her distinguished sons, is in his own words, "not to perpetuate his fame but to record her gratitude." At the same time, it is appropriate that some of the reasons for this gratitude should be made a part of the ceremony that does honor to the sentiments of the people and government of the State no less than to the public services of the great citizen to whom the original Colony gave birth.

The name of William Henry Harrison is inseparable from the momentous events of one of the most stirring and critical periods of our Country's existence. In reviewing his services and his contribution to the Republic, we come into intimate association with names, personages, and events that adorn some of the most brilliant pages of our history. Men of great intellect, builders of empire, the good and the evil, the patriot and the traitor, the soldier and the statesman, pass in review. Woven into the fabric of national progress, policies, growth, and development, there is revealed enduring evidences of the steady hand, the brave heart, and the clear head that distinguished him

[117]

as leader, soldier, statesman, and citizen. In imagination, he becomes vital and pulsing, for he lives, not alone in bronze and stone, but in the immortal record of history and in the hearts of an ever grateful people. For the sake of continuity, it is fitting to begin this appreciation of him by a reference to his birth and early life in the Colony of Virginia. Historians do not weary of paying tribute to the families of the Colony, who, preserving their English customs, possessed with wealth, and established in palatial homes and estates along the James, constituted under the then existing government a real aristocracy. Among them, the Harrison family was recognized as second to none. With a proud ancestry and related by marriage to nearly all of the distinguished names, they took a leading place in each generation. It is sufficient to illustrate by the well-known fact that Benjamin Harrison, the father of William Henry Harrison, was one of the dominant members of the first two Continental Congresses and a signer of the immortal Declaration. He had been a member of the House of Burgesses and later was speaker of the House of Delegates. He was twice elected Governor of Virginia, and in various other ways, he rendered services of the first order to the State and the Nation. Of such ancestry, William Henry Harrison was born at his father's home of Berkeley, Charles City County, Virginia, February 9, 1773. If it thus appears that he was born with the proverbial silver spoon, it will presently be seen that nothing which he ever achieved was handed on a silver tray, but rather that it was his fate to drink the symbolic cup to its bitter dregs.

His education in youth was such as his native State afforded. That he did not fail to improve his opportunities is demonstrated by a cultural and a classical background which gave charm and richness to his writings and speeches in after life. His father destined him for the medical profession. Though this did not accord with his wishes, he dutifully entered upon his studies with distinguished practitioners among his father's friends. At the age of nineteen, while so engaged in Philadelphia, he received news of his father's death. While this bereavement brought poignant grief, it gave him the release that he desired from a distasteful profession and left him free to follow his preference for a military career. Between General Richard Henry Lee, who encouraged him, and Robert Morris, his guardian, who opposed his wishes, he chose the advice of the former. It was not difficult to induce President Washington, his father's friend, to appoint him as an Ensign in the First Infantry.

It would be tedious to trace his early career as a young officer of the Army, yet he was a part of thrilling adventure and strange environment that called forth the highest qualities of courage, self-control, physical endurance, mental ability, and adherence to high standards of moral values, often not in harmony with his environment. He joined his Company at Fort Washington, on the site of Cincinnati, just after General St. Clair's tragic defeat by the Indians on November 9, 1791. The sight of the shattered and demoralized survivors, with their tales of hardship, danger, and death, was a violent and discouraging introduction to the details of military life. Yet, he was quickly called upon to lead a party through the savage-infested wilderness on a mission of relief.

So acute became the situation with the Indians and the British in the Northwest, that Congress authorized President Washington to raise an army for the protection of the settlers. He assigned General Anthony Wayne to the command and the troops were assembled at Pittsburgh in 1792. It was here that an event occurred which constituted the first step in the long road that was to lead Harrison to the pinnacle of fame and honor. Any general officer would probably agree that the first requisite of an Aide-de-camp is that of being a gentleman. Influenced, no doubt, by Ensign Harrison's birth and breeding, General Wayne selected him as an aide, notwithstanding his lack of experience and training as an officer. Subsequent events showed that the General made no mistake. During the two years that followed, by close association with Wayne in the process of converting raw levies into disciplined and trained soldiers, equal to the demands of the most arduous service, Harrison learned from a master in the practical school of his profession. With Wayne's brilliant victory over the British and the Indians at the battle of Fallen Timbers, he secured the northwest country to the United States and actually ended the war of the Revolution. Lieutenant Harrison's conduct in the battle merited and received the commendation of his Commander.

Upon the death of Wayne shortly afterwards, Harrison, who had been successively promoted to the grade of Captain, was given command of Fort Washington. Here, he took another step that was destined to shape his career by marrying the daughter of Judge John Charles Symmes in 1795. All accounts agree that the Judge was opposed to the marriage, but he soon became so reconciled that he ever after used his powerful influence in favor of his son-in-law. Indeed, without such influence, his next stride of progress might not have been possible.

With the suspension of hostilities, Harrison grew dissatisfied with army life, or at least made plans that were better suited to his condition. He, therefore, resigned in 1798. Through the help of an old friend in Congress, the Honorable Robert Goodloe Harper, to whom he applied, he was appointed Secretary of the Territory of the Northwest July 6, 1798, a little more than a month after his resignation was accepted. Within two more months, the Territory was advanced to the second grade of government and became entitled to a delegate in Congress. Governor St. Clair's faction advanced Arthur St. Clair, Jr., the Attorney General of the Territory, while Judge Symme's following, called the "Virginia Group," supported Harrison. There was bitter personal and political controversy between the parties and the contest was intense. In the legislative vote, Harrison won by 11 to 10.

Through his father's name and his personal associations, he found many friends among the most influential men in Congress. He at once devoted himself to the most urgent needs of his constituents. Indeed, throughout his public services, he declared that his highest duty was to act in conformity with their wishes. At that time, under the law, no tract of public land less than six hundred and forty acres could be purchased and only one-half of a township could be purchased in tracts less than three miles square. The land was sold at auction at a few distant places, at a minimum price of two dollars per acre, to be paid within one year. As a result, the public domain went into the hands of wealthy speculators and the poor man could not afford to own a home, or was compelled to buy at an exorbitant price. Delegate Harrison endeavored to amend the law so that land could be sold in one hundred and sixty acre lots, at places accessible to the settlers, with four years for payment. The opposition was so great that he could secure the sale of a minimum tract of three hundred and twenty acres only, but his other efforts were successful. Even this much attracted thousands of settlers and began a continuing policy of ameliorating their condition. He also did much to confirm old titles, reform the judiciary, and partition the Territory, about which there existed acute political controversy. The act creating the new Territory of Indiana was approved May 13, 1800, and within a few days, Harrison was appointed Governor. No doubt his experience and the knowledge he had shown in Congress of the conditions in the Northwest were used by his friends to persuade President Adams to make the appointment. It cannot be said that he was allied to any political party and he always denied the allegation of his enemies in after years, that he was a Federalist. He spent some time with relatives in Virginia after Congress adjourned and did not reach Vincennes, the Capital of the Territory, till June 10, 1801.

At the time of his appointment, he was twenty-seven years old. The duties of Governor brought about a violent change in his relationships and his status towards other men. Prior to this time, he had few occasions to thwart the wishes of others and to create enmities. On the contrary, his pleasing personality, his broad sympathies and his many opportunities for helpfulness, individually and *en masse*, had added to his inherited friendships. Indeed, the men who most staunchly supported his interests in his subsequent career were the friends acquired previous to this time. Now, he was entering upon a life of unending strife. His success was established and ever after his career demonstrated the truth that "Success is like the sunshine; it brings the vipers out." The conditions in the Territory in themselves were fruitful of conflict. There was an obsession of land hunger among the whites who demanded the extinction of the Indian titles. On the contrary, the Indians, encouraged by the British, determined to stop the progress of the whites and repudiated the alleged claims under the treaties. Indian raids and retaliation by the whites were of constant occurrence. The dual office of Civil Governor and Superintendent of Indian

Affairs, with unlimited and absolute powers in each case, brought him into constant conflict with both elements. There devolved upon him the adoption of laws from the various State codes, appointment of officials, creation of political sub-divisions, military preparations, execution of the laws, adjustment of claims, public land sales, salt leases, and, eventually, dealing with a legislature and territorial politics. Even Aaron Burr's activities intruded upon his sphere of responsibility. He succeeded in having grants of land devoted to the support of schools. He advocated military training in schools, and upon his recommendation, a township near Vincennes was set aside for a school for military instruction. He was reappointed twice by President Jefferson and once by President Madison, thus holding office for twelve years. For a short period, the District of Louisiana was placed under his jurisdiction and he received the thanks of the people when his administration of its affairs terminated. During all this time, his enemies increased. Charges were continually brought against him and refuted. Towards the end, he was constantly on the defensive. His most delicate and responsible task, however, was in relation to the Indians. The entire Territory was occupied by several tribes, including the strong Miamis and the aggressive Shawnees. A few were friendly but all were restive under their sense of injustice from the whites. The Chiefs were generally able men who knew their rights and had the courage to uphold them. They came freely to Governor Harrison with their troubles, including the sale of liquor that was demoralizing and destroying the tribes; the unjust administration of law by which Indians were invariably punished for crimes against whites while the latter were never held for crimes against the Indians; the invasion by the whites of the hunting grounds, reserved by treaty to the Indians; and the continued pressure to extinguish the title to the lands owned by the Indians. At the same time, the whites were pressing their demands for more land for speculation and settlement in order to increase the population for an advance to statehood. President Jefferson initiated an aggressive policy of obtaining all of the Indian lands and either civilizing them or driving them beyond the Mississippi. President Madison adhered to this policy even though he was less aggressive in its execution. Governor Harrison sympathized deeply with the Indians and endeavored to ameliorate their condition by stopping the sale of liquor and by honestly administering the gratuities and supplies furnished by the Government. In the last analysis, however, he was but the instrumentality of an inexorable civilization, and in carrying out the President's policy, it devolved upon him to find ways and means to obtain the lands peacefully, if possible, and forcibly, if necessary. It would be a long recital to describe the conferences that he held with the chiefs and the tribes, the resistance that he encountered, the expedients that he employed, the courage and tact that he displayed, and the hostility that was engendered in the process by which, in nine years, he obtained cessions from the Indians to the United States of seventy million acres of the choicest land on the Continent. It is doubtful whether there was another man who combined the personal qualities, knowledge, and experience requisite to the fulfillment of so gigantic and delicate an undertaking. This alone would have justified the name given by his admiring friends of Father of the Northwest. It will presently appear, however, that holding was even more difficult than obtaining.

The British, who had never relinquished their intention of retaining much of the Northwest, in spite of the treaty after the Revolution, were not slow in taking advantage of the resentment and hostility which the loss of their lands created among the Indians. There is no doubt that the British agents, with or without the instructions of the government, incited the chiefs to revenge and gave all the aid at their disposal. At the height of these events, there appeared upon the scene two of the most significant characters in the annals of the Indian race. These were the Prophet and Tecumseh, twin brothers of the Shawnee tribe. The one assuming the rôle of a Messiah, represented the Deity and worked upon the credulity and imagination of the tribes by picturing a golden era before the white man came and by proposing to restore it through the extermination of the whites. The latter was a practical leader of men, brave, brilliant, eloquent, and dominating. They assumed the leadership of all the tribes of the continent and demanded that no treaty be considered valid unless approved by the Indians as a race, to whom the hunting grounds belonged in common. Following a period of raids and depredations upon the settlers, Governor Harrison demanded that the Prophet and his followers remove from their town of Tippecanoe, on the Wabash, to which place the Governor had previously forced them to go. This, the Prophet defiantly declined to do. Taking advantage of the absence of Tecumseh, the real military leader, who had gone to organize the southern tribes, Governor Harrison with a force of about one thousand regulars, Kentucky volunteers and Indiana militia, advanced against the Prophet in compliance with orders from the War Department. He reached the Prophet's town on the evening of November 6, 1811. Efforts to induce him to leave peaceably were insultingly rejected. Before daylight on March 7, the Indians attacked Governor Harrison's camp. His dispositions had been skillfully made and his personal conduct of the defense showed his knowledge of command.

In a short time the Indians were driven off. The victory, however, cost nearly one-fifth of the troops in killed and wounded. While the men fought bravely and were well led by their officers, it was unquestionably Governor Harrison's preparations, foresight, wisdom, coolness, and courage that prevented Tippecanoe from being another Harmer or St. Clair massacre. The troops gave him full credit; and while his enemies later tried to slander him, their falsehoods only redounded to his fame. He became a national hero and was lauded by Legislatures and Governors, and the President in his message to Congress.

Again events culminated to create a new phase of his unique career. However successful and creative may have been his life as a civil administrator, he was innately a soldier. The call to arms held for him always the strongest appeal. The outrages by the British government, which had continued since the Revolution, came to a culmination shortly after the chastisement of the Prophet. War was declared against Great Britain, June 18, 1812. Governor Harrison at once began efforts to secure a general officer's commission in the Army. There were many complications in his activities, but largely, no doubt, through the Kentucky troops and Henry Clay, he was appointed a Major General of the Kentucky militia. These troops held him in such high esteem that they later refused to let another officer supplant him over them. In the meantime, he showed a clear grasp of the military situation, indicating a plan of campaign and pointing out the danger and effect of losing Mackinac, Fort Dearborn, and Detroit. His wisdom was amply vindicated with the surrender of General Hull at Detroit, August 15, before the War Department could organize a force for his relief. With his Kentucky commission, he set about organizing a force to relieve Fort Wayne and reinforce Detroit. While these plans were in progress, he was commissioned a Brigadier General in the regular army and on September 17, he was given full command by the President of all the troops in the Northwest. He at once submitted a plan of campaign for the recovery of Detroit and began raising and assembling the troops. The magnitude of this task is inconceivable in view of the untamed character of the volunteers, the absence of roads in an impassable wilderness, the lack of supplies, munitions, and transportation, and the lateness of the season. He accomplished all that was humanly possible. Several expeditions were sent against the most dangerous tribes who were allied with the British. It became evident, however, that the land expedition could not be executed that winter. On December 12, he wrote his estimate of the situation to the Secretary of War, recommending that the winter campaign be abandoned and that a fleet be built to gain control of Lake Erie. This would permit an expedition by water to attack the British in their rear and take the war into Canada. It appears that this view had been expressed by him some years before when war with Great Britain had been considered imminent. General Hull had also made a similar recommendation. The final adoption of the plan, however, may fairly be credited to General Harrison. He was now experiencing to the full the consequences of unpreparedness for war. Notwithstanding boasting in Congress prior to hostilities that Canada would at once fall into our hands, the events of the campaign demonstrated the incapacity and blindness of the government since the Revolution in neglecting to organize the land forces for defense and the War Department for functioning in war. Meanwhile, he constructed forts and bases for the protection of supplies and assembly points and continued his efforts for the land campaign. An event now took place that put an end to such a possibility. The troops for the operation were being assembled between the Sandusky and the Maumee rivers. General Winchester, commanding the column on the Maumee, contrary to General Harrison's latest orders, had advanced to the rapids. From there he sent a detachment of several hundred men to protect the settlement at Frenchtown on the River Raisin. At first the troops were successful against the Indians, but after remaining two days, they were attacked on January 22, 1813, by a superior force of British and Indians under General Proctor. Nearly all were captured and slaughtered by the Indians. As soon as General Harrison heard of the movement he acted promptly to send reinforcements and proceeded himself to the rapids, but the distance was too great for timely help.

On February 27, 1813, President Madison appointed him a Major General and he was confirmed March 1 when he ceased to be Governor of Indiana. In addition to the troops in the field, he assumed command of the Eighth Military District which comprised all the western theater of operations. He was given complete and independent powers, as was the case with his appointment as Governor. There were constant troubles and changes with the militia and volunteers, but his indefatigable activity in recruiting and his personal prestige with them enabled him to maintain his contingents in training.

In April, the British General Proctor advanced with a force of one thousand whites and one thousand two hundred Indians to attack Fort Meigs which General Harrison had built at the Maumee Rapids. Upon learning of the movement, General Harrison went to the fort and took personal charge of the defense. From May 1 to 9, the fort was violently attacked, but due to his leadership and skill, all efforts failed and the British withdrew.

Since General Harrison's recommendation as to the advance by Lake Erie, there had been three Secretaries of War. The last, Armstrong, decided in March, 1813, to adopt the plan. Accordingly, Commodore Perry began the construction of a fleet at Erie. The composition of the troops and the details of embarkation were decided by General Harrison, whose views differed materially from those of the Secretary of War.

In the meantime, another event demonstrated the wisdom and sound judgment of the commander. Fort Stephenson, a supply base at Lower Sandusky, was garrisoned by less than two hundred men under Captain Croghan. General Harrison had directed him to withdraw, if the British approached, but to defend his position against Indians alone. The officer suddenly found himself threatened by British and Indians and decided to remain and defend himself. The assault was made August 1 and was repulsed by the garrison. General Harrison, who was nine miles away with a small detachment, was later criticized by his enemies for not going to Croghan's relief. Had he done so with a force too small to fight its way, he no doubt would have been massacred by a large body of Indians under Tecumseh who were waiting for such an opportunity. Both his officers and Captain Croghan sustained his action.

Through his incessant zeal and activity, he accumulated the forces for the land expedition by the time that Perry had constructed his fleet. The command consisted mainly of a few regulars, Kentucky infantry under Governor Shelby and a Kentucky regiment of mounted infantry under Colonel R. W. Johnson. The naval engagement took place September 10, and Perry sent to Harrison the immortal dispatch, "We have met the enemy and they are ours." The embarkation followed as rapidly as possible and on September 27 the army of five thousand men appeared

[129]

before the British fort at Malden, across the river from Detroit. It was found that Proctor had begun his retreat up the Thames three days before and thus had a long start. After occupying Detroit, the pursuit began. On October 5, the enemy was found occupying a strong position between the river and an impassable swamp, with the Indians beyond the swamp. General Harrison promptly made his dispositions for attack and, taking advantage of an open formation of the British, ordered the mounted infantry to charge. The battle was over in a few minutes. The entire British force, except the Commander, was captured. Tecumseh was killed and the Indians dispersed. General Harrison was entitled to the full credit of his leadership. Again, the Nation resounded with his praise. Illuminations and parades took place in all the principal cities. The one in Richmond was especially brilliant and enthusiastic. Again tributes were paid to him by Governors, the President, and the representatives of the people. He was called the "Washington of the West." In after years his enemies attempted to deprive him of his well-earned laurels, but Shelby, Perry, Johnson, and all others concerned manfully came to his defense.

After the Battle of the Thames, General Harrison established a military occupation and civil government in conjunction with Commodore Perry, in the captured territory. He then proceeded to the Niagara frontier with one thousand one hundred men. Before he accomplished any plan on the Niagara, he was ordered with his troops to Sackett's Harbor where he was relieved by the Secretary of War and ordered to his Military District. On the way, he received ovations at New York, Philadelphia, and Baltimore. This virtually ended his military career. The Secretary of War became hostile to him; and after repeated slights, he resigned May 11, 1814. In his arduous service, he had overcome the most baffling difficulties; he had won every battle when defeat of our forces elsewhere was the rule; he possessed the affection and confidence of all the troops who served under him; he had received the plaudits of the people, Legislatures, Governors, and the President; he had the unswerving friendship of such men as Shelby, Perry, and McArthur, who thought that he should be placed in supreme command of the army; but he had incurred the jealousy and hostility of politicians and officers less successful and of contractors who were thwarted by him in their nefarious profiteering. He was doomed to spend the rest of his life defending his conduct and his honor against these and his political rivals. There is no doubt, however, that his subsequent career in public life and his eventual rise to the highest office were a direct result of his military achievements.

He now devoted himself to his personal affairs at North Bend, which were in a deplorable condition, due to his public service and the recent death of his father-in-law. While the Secretary of War was no doubt glad to be rid of him as an officer, his services were indispensable in dealing with the Indians. In 1814 and 1815, he was appointed head of commissions to make treaties with the troublesome tribes. In both cases, he resisted successfully the policy to acquire more land. The first concluded peace and the second ratified the treaties made prior to the war. Between 1815 and 1817 an investigation was conducted by Congress at the instigation of his enemies, of his dealings with contractors. He was vindicated and eulogized on the floor, as having protected the interests of the Government. Between 1814 and 1818, a Joint Resolution in Congress to award the thanks of Congress and medals to General Harrison and Governor Shelby was used by his enemies in an effort to ruin him. His protests and the evidence presented resulted in his being accorded by Congress full credit for his military qualities as a commander. The bill was passed by both Houses and approved by the President. Antaeus-like, he rose stronger after each blow. While the investigation was in progress his friends urged him to accept the nomination for Congress in order that he might be present in that body to defend himself. He was elected and took his seat December 2, 1816. His labors were devoted to land questions, reforms in the military system of which he had been a victim, and the relief of soldiers and their families whose welfare was near his heart throughout his life. He advocated just compensation for veterans, relief of all in distressed circumstances, regardless of the cause, and a bounty of land. His experience led him to propose a revision of the militia laws so as to provide for the military training of the youth in schools and the control of training of the militia by the Government. His ideas were regarded as visionary and were ignored. A century was to pass, bringing the penalty of neglect, before his wisdom was recognized and his recommendations became a part of the Government's military policy. He was also deeply concerned about internal improvements, and among the projects advocated by him was a canal by the rapids of the Ohio at Louisville, which has been realized only within a few years. He was re-elected in 1817. Again he advocated the same legislation as before. On the resolution to extend thanks to Jackson he proposed an amendment, disapproving of the execution of Ambrister as being contrary to law. His views as to the inalienable rights of slave holders and slave states were based upon his interpretation of the Constitution. In both cases he was destined to suffer for his courage. During the session of 1817–1818, he opposed increasing the pay of Congressmen from six to nine dollars per day till the needs of veterans and their families had been supplied. On January 6, 1818, he finally proposed an amendment that the increase should only take effect with the succeeding Congress. Again his views were not shared by other members. During this time he endeavored to secure the appointment as Secretary of War and as a member of a mission to Russia, but was unsuccessful.

After the expiration of his term in Congress he was elected to the Senate of Ohio in 1819. Here again his interpretation of the Constitution, as it applied to a United States Bank, and his vote in favor of selling the services of minor offenders instead of confining them in jail, were the cause of attacks on him in after years. In 1820, he was defeated for Governor of Ohio, and in 1821 he was defeated for United States Senator. In 1823 and 1824 he tried repeatedly to induce the President to appoint him as Minister to Mexico, giving as a reason, his financial needs. In 1825 he was successful in his efforts to be elected United States Senator. Here he was active in the support of measures for internal improvement, especially rivers, canals, and roads. He became Chairman of the Committee on Military Affairs and spent much time on measures to ameliorate the condition of officers and soldiers, to increase the pay of junior officers and enlisted men, to relieve veterans, and to adjust claims for pensions. He defeated an iniquitous measure to abolish the grade of Major General, commanding the army, and his masterly report remains a classic in its clear conception of the proper administration of the War Department. In no way related to this principle, he advanced his claims to succeed to a vacancy of Major General, but was unsuccessful. One of his deepest disappointments of this period was the failure of Ohio and Virginia to support his efforts to become candidate for Vice President in 1828. For this, he was compensated in a measure, through Clay and other friends, in obtaining the appointment as Minister to Colombia. President Adams is said to have been unfriendly to Senator Harrison and to have made the appointment in deference to the entire Cabinet and to the delegations of Ohio, Kentucky, and Indiana. His financial condition at this time was peculiarly desperate and he hoped to find some relief in his pay and allowances.

He reached Bogotá on February 5, 1829, and was received on the twenty-seventh. On March 8, four days after President Jackson's inauguration, he was recalled. It is not difficult to attribute this action of Jackson's to his resentment in the Ambrister case, though he based it solely upon the connection of the previous administration with the Panama Mission. Minister Harrison remained in his office till the arrival of his successor on September 26. The disturbed conditions in Colombia gave the Minister ample material for his energies and his sentiments. His passionate love of freedom and constitutional government aroused his sympathies for the unfortunate and destitute people. He kept his Government accurately informed as to the trend towards a monarchy, involving other Latin-American states. Ultimately, he aroused the resentment of General Bolivar's Government and of those foreign representatives who aided and abetted its ambitions. After his relinquishment of office, he was subjected to indignities and embarrassment that were not redressed by the United States, some of whose agents were in part responsible for neglect of his needs. The day after he took his leave of the Government, he addressed a personal letter to General Bolivar which must ever live as a classic in literature and an expression of the noblest spirit and loftiest patriotism. While Minister Harrison was much criticized for his temerity, there is ample evidence that his purpose was accomplished, for, thereafter, the policy of Bolivar underwent a complete change.

In April, 1830, after a journey at his own expense, General Harrison, as he must hereafter be called, returned to his farm at North Bend. Family reverses added to his financial embarrassment, and he found himself heavily in debt. The farm was his only means of livelihood, and he endeavored, by scientific methods, to increase its earning power. He even contemplated migrating to the Mexican frontier in search of a new opportunity. In 1834, however, his friends secured his appointment as Clerk of the Court of Common Pleas of Hamilton County. During all these vicissitudes, his patience and fortitude never deserted him and his latch string was ever out to old comrades of the war and friends of better days. His thoughts turned constantly to a return to public life, but his efforts were unsuccessful. In 1831 he was defeated for the United States Senate, and his friends did not support him in his ambition to be Governor or Congressman. His activities, however, kept him before the public, and among minor evidences of recognition was his appointment as a member of the Board of Visitors to West Point in 1832.

Destiny was now hastening his career to its culmination. It was, however, an assisted destiny, for he lost no opportunity of asking for what he wanted and seeking the help of his friends. While he now aspired to a seat in the United States Senate, his friends were placing their eyes on a higher goal. In December, 1834, the *Pennsylvania Intelligencer* boldly suggested him for the Presidency. The complexity of the political situation at this time forbids its analysis in this paper.

On the whole, there was a general revolt against President Jackson, his policies and his arbitrary exercise of power. In spite of the sound arguments presented by him during his first term against a President's succeeding himself, he had procured his reelection and now he was charged with designating Van Buren as his successor. There were, then, no sectional lines in politics. Groupings appeared on various issues, all opposed to the administration but at variance with each other on other questions of the day. Largely, also, there was the age-old contest between the outs and the ins. From this heterogeneous mass, there was crystallized a party called National-Republican. The different groupings shared in common the old term of Whig, originally applied in opprobrium by the British to the patriots. Clay, Webster, and Calhoun, as well as other able men, were proposed by their friends for the nomination by the Whigs. Objection was made to General Harrison by some of the party that he had not been sufficiently active in, or acquainted with, politics and was not familiar with the issues. His age and alleged ill health were added to the pretense that he had not earned the place by service to the party.

General Harrison now became very aggressive, personally and through his friends. Like the warrior that he was by nature, he scented the battle, and he did not underestimate its fierceness nor shrink from the conflict. He cleverly avoided exposing himself to controversial issues that would give his opponents the advantage, and in his talks dwelt upon the military campaigns which so many of his hearers had shared with him. At the same time he returned savagely the thrusts made at his record. During 1835, Harrison sentiment grew rapidly and in various parts of the country, he received the nomination of local conventions. A powerful element in the party was the Antimasonic group, and General Harrison's progress received strong impetus when the Antimasonic Convention at Harrisburg, on December 14, 1835, nominated him over the Webster faction. Similar action occurred in New York. Virginia was divided in her allegiance between Harrison and White of Tennessee and placed both names on the ticket. It will be understood that, at this time, the Whigs did not consider a national convention truly representative of the people and nominations were by states. In the meantime, General Harrison was called upon to express his views upon some of the principal issues, such as appointment of Masons to office, the tariff, the distribution to the states of the receipts from sales of public lands, public improvements in states by the Federal Government, the re-charter of the United States Bank, expunging the records of Congress and slavery. In general, his views had been made of record in his public life. His replies might well have alienated groups in his own party; but he was frank and unequivocal, basing his conclusions upon the Constitution. The candidates who survived for the opposition to the administration were Harrison, Webster, and White. There being no convention for nomination, three candidates were in the field. Harrison received the electoral votes of Vermont, New Jersey, Delaware, Maryland, Kentucky, Ohio, and Indiana, amounting to 73. White won Georgia and Tennessee, while Webster had only Massachusetts. Van Buren won with 170. In some states his popular vote but slightly exceeded that cast for Harrison. The latter displayed such strength that, in looking ahead, the consensus of opinion was expressed by Seward when he said that Harrison should be the next "candidate by continuation." What Tippecanoe was to his brilliant military career, the political campaign of 1836 was to that which followed.

We now approach a culmination so dramatic and picturesque, so stirring and unprecedented, as to overshadow the hitherto remarkable life of a remarkable man. Van Buren had triumphed, but the forces of the opposition intended not only to make him pay dearly for his victory but to organize an invincible host against his future hopes.

For the sake of historical clarity it is appropriate to depart from a strict sequence of events and illuminate the period as a whole.

The political terminology is itself confusing. The Republican party of Jefferson became the Democratic party of Jackson. The party policies purported to promote the welfare of the agricultural and laboring masses. They opposed the high tariff protecting industry and making the poor instead of the rich pay the cost of the Government, the federal financial system enriching bankers and speculators, and subsidies to favored enterprises.

The Federalists of Hamilton had become the Whigs or National-Republican party. Their theories of Government favored a high tariff, promoting manufacturing and trade, sound currency, the reëstablishment of the United States Bank, subsidies to business and shipping, and public improvements to promote trade. Webster was the acknowledged champion of the interests and was not only a stipendiary of the United States Bank but the recipient of a substantial income from wealthy sources. Clay was likewise a leader in this school.

Calhoun represented the planters of the South who tried to unite with them the farmers of the West and the laborers of the East. He proclaimed the fundamental doctrine enunciated by Jefferson and Jackson that there was an inevitable conflict and antagonism between the necessities of agriculture and labor on the one side and the interest of capital and industry on the other.

The party of the soil and the shop had gained the ascendency and under Jackson became strongly intrenched. The

[138]

party of the interests saw that the only way to a restoration of power was through the methods and appeals adopted by their antagonists. This explains the paradox of seeking a candidate from the farmer class who was *available* as distinguished from the acknowledged leaders who were eminently *qualified*. Throughout the campaign, great stress was laid by the Whigs upon minor and almost irrelevant issues to the exclusion of basic party policies. Thus while the party wore the clothing of the agricultural sheep, it concealed the capitalistic wolf. However much or little Harrison may have understood the party designs, they were soon revealed when on coming into power it forced Tyler to veto two bills for the reëstablishment of the United States Bank. The paradox was further extended by the fact that the standard bearer of the party of the people was himself a so-called aristocrat who, in all but politics, was allied to the class of luxury.

It cannot be supposed, however, that any duplicity attached to Harrison's attitude. Throughout his life, he was essentially a soldier. His viewpoint was national and not sectional. His loyalty was first to the country which he placed above party prejudices and aspirations. He was too honest to lend himself to selfish schemes and too shrewd to suffer others to lead him into dubious ways. Had he lived, he would have used his power to guide his party to his country's good.

In the ranks of the Whigs were in addition to master leaders like Webster, Clay, and White, such shrewd political strategists as Thurlow Weed, Penrose, Seward, Fillmore, Henry A. Wise, and Greeley, as well as many less known but not less able tacticians and organizers. In the closing period of President Jackson's administration, his hard money policy was charged with having caused a precarious money situation and financial stringency. His order removing the money of the Treasury from the United States Bank, after a Secretary of the Treasury had been dismissed for refusing to do so, was continually attacked. In 1837, a financial panic spread through the land. Banks failed in great numbers, business firms became bankrupt, commerce and industry were paralyzed, wages declined, and unemployment prevailed. While these evils were capitalized and charged to the administration, a fairer estimate was made by Thomas Cooper of South Carolina when he said, "To be sure, over-trading and gambling speculation will account for three-fourths of the present distress, but no one can be blind to the effects produced by the desperate ignorance of the last President." In preparing for the campaign of 1840, the Whigs had three prominent possibilities, though several lesser ones were advanced by their friends. Harrison's strength assured him of a place before the party. Clay had a large following and expected to be the candidate, while Webster's friends held out little hope. The leaders decided to unite on one man and not fritter away their votes on several candidates. The first significant move was a state Whig Convention at Pittsburgh in June, 1838. Harrison was nominated for President, but the convention agreed to support any candidate named at the National Convention. In spite of Clay's desire not to be presented too soon, a movement in New York in his favor was inaugurated in the summer of 1837. Webster's friends also were active. Again the Antimasons asserted themselves by holding a National Convention in Washington, September 12, 1837, and proposed but did not nominate Harrison. The Whig leaders now decided to call a National Convention at Harrisburg in December, 1839. The Antimasons again met near Philadelphia November 13, 1838, and definitely nominated Harrison for President. Clay's friends became equally active and both he and Harrison gained in strength. Webster's name was withdrawn with his approval, and some of his supporters in New York advanced the candidacy of General Winfield Scott. By the time that the Convention met at Harrisburg on December 4, 1839, the Clay supporters felt that he would receive the nomination. What followed was in the realm of high politics, guided by the most astute and experienced hands in that highly technical field. In the end, Harrison received 148 votes, Clay 90, and Scott 16. In spite of disappointments, all now united to support the candidate. Both Webster and Calhoun had declined to be considered for Vice President with Harrison. Tyler was named, possibly in accordance with promises made to the Virginia leaders in connection with a previous election of a United States Senator from that State. Although Clay had written in the most unselfish strain, agreeing to abide by the will of the Convention, his disappointment and resentment appear to have been expressed by him in the most violent manner. His friends and others inveighed against the choice while the administration forces were delighted by the prospect of an easy victory.

With the nomination, the battle was now joined. In all probability the campaign might have followed the normal course of the preceding one with the advantage on the side of the office-holding spoils administration, had not a trivial event transformed Harrison from a candidate of a party into a candidate of the people. In the endeavor of the administration organs to discredit him by ridicule and contempt, the *Baltimore Republican* said, "Give him a barrel of hard cider and a pension of two thousand a year, and our word for it, he will sit the remainder of his days in a log cabin by the side of a 'sea coal' fire and study moral philosophy." As if by a miracle, this opened the flood gates of the most extraordinary hysteria and excitement that has been known in this country. The Whigs, seeing its appeal to the people, presented him as the simple farmer who lived in a log cabin. It excited the imagination of the masses who were poor and of the settlers of the great Northwest who resented the slur upon their homes. The log cabin became the symbol of the campaign and its accompaniments, the coon skin and the cider barrel, vied with it in popularity. Cider became the national drink. The Harrison ball was started rolling and was reproduced in every place. The farmer's shirt and dress became almost a uniform of the people. Hundreds of wagons and teams paraded everywhere as emblems of the farm. The fame of the Candidate's achievements in the field was revived and "Old Tip" became an idol. The Nation burst into song with "Old Tip" and hard cider as the principal theme. Scores of ballads were sung to the most popular tunes, extolling his virtues and his exploits. So contagious was the enthusiasm that even the young people of the opposite party could not refrain from taking part, to the great displeasure of their elders. One who did not shout and sing for "Tippecanoe and Tyler too" was lonesome indeed. The complete organization of committees carried out a program of parades, conventions, and rallies in every city, town, and hamlet. The entire population participated in these holidays and people would travel for miles in their wagons to enjoy the pageant. Without the sources of amusement that have since been developed, they found in these celebrations the excitement that they craved. Banners, mottoes, almanacs, newspapers, and every conceivable device spread the propaganda of the party. For the first time, women took an active interest; and while their participation was confined to

viewing the parades from windows and waving handker-
chiefs, there was no doubt as to their influence on the men.
The candidate was stressed as a poor and honorable farmer.
The more that calumny and abuse were heaped upon him
by the administration party, the more the people rallied
to his defense and denounced the autocratic and oppressive
office-holders. Like a great avenging wave, they rolled
up to overwhelm the party who for twelve years they
regarded as having trampled upon their rights. Harrison
was continually compelled to defend himself against
charges of cowardice, incapacity as a commander, Federal-
ism, advocating slavery for white people, profiteering from
contractors, abolitionism, and various other offenses.
Old antagonisms and prejudices in the party were buried
for the moment. The motto of Wise, "Union of the Whigs
for the sake of the Union," was enthusiastically adopted.
Clay received an ovation in Nashville, the stronghold of
his mortal enemy, Jackson; Webster, the abolitionist,
was acclaimed in Richmond, where he made four of his
captivating speeches during one visit, and Wise put aside
his prejudice against soldier Presidents, no doubt, for the
sake of his friend Tyler.

There was much confusion of terminology in the two
parties. The Jacksonians called themselves Democrats,
though they were charged with having all the character-
istics of the old Federalists. Harrison always proclaimed
himself a Democratic Republican, but the party called
itself National Republican. All united as Whigs. By the
time that the Democratic Convention met at Baltimore,
May 5, 1840, and renominated Van Buren, the country was
mad with the Whig campaign. Platforms had no appeal
amid the din of songs and cool reasoning as to issues was
well-nigh impossible. Yet Clay, Webster, and other
stalwarts stirred their hearers with their eloquence and

their logic. The party doctrines were best set forth by Clay when he visited his birthplace at Taylorsville, Va., June 27, 1840. They were essentially :
Ineligibility to the office of President after one term.
Limited exercise of the veto.
Restricting dismissal from office.
Congressional control of the Treasury.
Ineligibility of Members of Congress to appointment to office.
A stabilized currency.
Reform in administering the public lands.
Protection of American industry.
Economy in public expenditures.
State construction of public improvements.
Constitutional rights of slave States.
The candidate committed himself :
To confine his tenure of office to a single term.
To disclaim control over the Treasury.
Not to influence elections through office-holders.
To limit the veto power to acts that were unconstitutional, or unjust to States or individuals, or that required an expression of the will of the people.
To be governed by the Constitution and the necessities of the Government upon the recharter of a United States Bank.
To recognize the constitutional rights of slave States and slave holders.
To give reasons for removals from office.
To refrain from initiating legislation.
To reform the abuses of Locofocoism and autocratic government.
His own speeches were few in number and confined to the scenes of his achievements in the Northwest. In these, he defended his record and reaffirmed his policies.

When the election returns were received, it was found that almost twice as many men voted in 1840 as in 1836. While Harrison received 1,275,000 votes, Van Buren received only 45,000 less. At the same time, Harrison received 234 electoral votes, while Van Buren had only 60. Neither Virginia nor South Carolina was carried for Harrison, though the former claimed him by birth and the latter had no reason to ally itself with Jackson's party. The party leaders at once set about the formation of a cabinet. It was soon found that with the election won, the various factions had no longer a common bond. A compromise cabinet was selected, but factions and sections felt slighted. Thus, the seeds of internal dissension were early sown. The President-elect gave no evidence of being conscious of the difficulties ahead of him and enjoyed to the full the adulation and honors heaped upon him. The excessive entertainment and excitement are said to have so weakened him physically as to render him an easy prey to disease.

The inauguration ceremony followed the conventional custom. His inaugural address breathed the same lofty patriotism, devotion to the Constitution, and vows for reform that had characterized his campaign speeches. Above all, he stressed the necessity for mutual respect and good will between the states as essential to the preservation of the union.

The White House became the usual scene of visitors, politicians, and office seekers. His time was absorbed largely by personal appeals to which he ever gave a sympathetic and willing ear. However, with Webster as Secretary of State, he initiated action to redeem his campaign pledges. On March 17, he called Congress in extra session for May 31 to consider the finances and currency of the country. On March 28, he was seized with a chill. Complications followed, and for a week he grew steadily worse, in spite of the best medical skill. The Nation breathlessly watched the bulletins and the people were stunned when on April 4 his death was announced. His last words expressed the supreme conviction of his life, "Sir, I wish you to understand the principles of the Government. I wish them carried out — I ask nothing more."

Following so closely upon the events of the campaign, it is doubtful whether the death of any other man has so profoundly moved the people. All partisanship was forgotten and the Nation mourned as a stricken and bereaved family. The funeral on April 8 was marked by all the circumstance and honor that a government could bestow. The body was placed in a vault in the Congressional Cemetery and was removed in June to North Bend. Here among the fields that he loved, on the spot that he called home, rested at last this great and good man in the fullness of years and of honors. The way of life, begun by the lad in old Virginia, had followed over the heights and the depths, through storm and sunshine, through good and evil days. Sustained and strengthened by rectitude, fidelity, courage, and fortitude, he had triumphed over every obstacle and had conquered every enemy save death. And who can tell, indeed, whether death itself was not a friend in disguise? Scarcely had his body been committed to the tomb, than there began the long series of controversies in the party of which President Tyler was the victim. It may be that his powers of control, his philosophical wisdom, and his popularity among the people would have guided the course of events to harmonious accomplishment, or it may be that, crushed by the load, his life would have come to a different end.

Looking back over a story so inadequately told, there are a few outstanding facts to be emphasized.

In his life of public service he probably held more offices of trust and responsibility than any other man whom our country has produced. Possessed of a laudable ambition and unbounded self-confidence, he did not hesitate to seek appointment or election to what he desired. He invariably succeeded in his duties, and in no way did he ever profit financially by public office. On the contrary, he lived and died in straightened circumstances, when, by taking advantage of his opportunities as a public official, he might have enriched himself.

He was kindly, unselfish, and hospitable to a degree worthy of his Virginia antecedents. He never forgot the men who served him or befriended him.

He understood the psychology of leadership. No other man ever so won the confidence and loyalty of the volunteer soldiers or accomplished so much with them. In the same way, he won the respect and admiration of the Indians, even when his duty compelled him to act contrary to their interests.

In character and tastes, he was essentially a soldier. The ethics of the military code dominated his conduct. By experience and study, he acquired a superior knowledge of the art of war, and by sound judgment and a certain natural aptitude, he applied his knowledge wisely. He never lost an engagement, nor did his subordinates fail when they obeyed his instructions.

He possessed a unique versatility of knowledge and in all things, he was practical. Behind his urbanity and simplicity, there was a vast resource of dynamic power, shrewdness, and common sense. In agriculture, the art of war, politics, and diplomacy, he rose above his compeers.

His early education and his reading gave him a cultivated mind and he was remarkably well grounded in literature and the classics. This was revealed in all of his public utterances and writings, which were adorned by the imagery and characters of the ancients. The purity of his diction and the eloquence of his composition were unexcelled in an age when oratory, rhetoric, and literature were at their height. Among the productions of his pen that will live are :

"A Discourse on the Aborigines of the Valley of the Ohio."

"The Tribute to Kosciusko on the Floor of Congress."

"The Appeal to General Bolivar."

"The Inaugural Address."

Some of his rivals criticized him as lacking in brilliancy. Unlike the flashing meteor that dazzles for a moment, his was the pure, serene beauty of the planet that illuminated the generation in which he lived, and continues to glow after he has passed below life's horizon.

He will ever be among the country's greatest soldiers, statesmen, and citizens; and the generations will not cease to cherish his memory in pride, reverence, and honor.

JOHN TYLER

President of the United States

1841–1845

CLAUDE G. BOWERS, *The Speaker*

FROM THE INTRODUCTION OF THE SPEAKER
by
GOVERNOR POLLARD

It is my pleasure to present to the audience our guests of honor on this occasion, Dr. Lyon Gardiner Tyler, President emeritus of the College of William and Mary, a distinguished son of President Tyler; Master Lyon Gardiner Tyler, age six, a grandson of the President, who will unveil the bust; Mrs. Pearl Tyler Ellis, a worthy daughter of a truly great man; Mrs. Alfred I. DuPont, a Virginian of noble birth and generous heart, who donated the bust of President Tyler; and Mr. Charles Keck, the sculptor, a favorite artist in Virginia, as attested by his many works found in the Old Dominion.

I wish also to acknowledge the presence here today of more than two score of the descendants of the man we honor on this occasion.

CHARLES KECK, *The Sculptor*

There is no surer way of keeping the fires of patriotism kindled than by recalling the lives and recounting the deeds of those who made our country great. Of these, John Tyler, as Representative, Senator, and President, was a man of courage and conviction. He helped to establish a firm financial system for his country. He successfully concluded Seminole War. He maintained peace between England and the United States by successful negotiation. His was the helping hand that brought Texas into the Union. This is the man we honor today.

The oration on this occasion is to be delivered by one whose historical works have placed him in the front rank of American writers of his day, a journalist, an editor, an author — an acknowledged student of the period of President Tyler. No man is better prepared to deliver an address on the life and times of John

MRS. ALFRED I. DUPONT, *The Donor*

Tyler than Claude G. Bowers, whom I now have the pleasure of presenting.

JOHN TYLER

ADDRESS BY

CLAUDE G. BOWERS

A LITTLE more than a decade before the Revolution, two ardent Virginia youths at William and Mary might have been seen almost any evening with their heads together in study. They were kindred spirits in their love of liberty and of the inalienable rights of man. Together, with flaming cheeks, they had listened in the Virginia Convention to the immortal eloquence of Patrick Henry. One was to become the greatest American political philosopher and the father of American democracy, and the other, one of his ablest and most trusted lieutenants, and the father of a future President whose bust we unveil today.

It was in the year that Jefferson and Madison, riding leisurely through New England, planned the organization of resistance to the domination of the Hamiltonians that John Tyler, to whom we pay tribute here today, was born. Reared in an atmosphere of culture and meditation, he was a precocious youth. He steeped himself in history, and thus found the background for his political convictions; in poetry, and thus cultivated the imagination and the gift of phrasing that was to give a literary flavor to his eloquence. The gentility of his manner was inherent, an inheritance of his blood, a reflection of his home. When at the age of seventeen he finished his course at Williamsburg, he possessed already the social charm, the suavity, and urbanity of a gentleman of the world. But his education was by no means confined to the curriculum of the college. From earliest childhood he had come under the influence of the remarkable man who was his father. The relations of Chatham and his brilliant son were not more influential in the burnishing of the genius of the younger Pitt than were those of Judge Tyler and the future President. By voice and pen the elder man impressed upon the scion of his house the fundamentals of the faith of Thomas Jefferson. There came a day when the ardent youth was to meet the great philosopher of his faith at his father's table, to come under the fascination of his personality, and to listen to an intimate political conversation he was to treasure always in his mind.

Thus on the very threshold of his life we find him firmly anchored to his creed in politics. He believed that men are the masters and not the slaves of government, that constitutions are the contracts binding on those in power; that states are entities with sovereign rights, that power should be diffused among the people and not centralized in some capital remote, that there are certain inalienable rights of men that governments dare not question, that any political action based on privilege is a usurpation and a crime, and that the function of government is to assure the liberties of the people, and to operate for the happiness of mankind. This was his political faith to which he clung tenaciously from the hour, when scarcely more than boy, he entered public life, until he laid his burdens down with death.

Since we are concerned primarily with his public life, it is interesting to glance at the equipment which was to make him the powerful and persuasive champion of any cause that he espoused. With strength, he had a winning personality which invited confidence. He was easy, graceful, and appealing; his urbanity drew men to him, and his dignity, without pose, saved him from the pawing of vulgarity. His voice in conference and conversation was ingratiating, and his features were lighted with the kindliness of true gentility. But nothing contributed more to the success of his leadership than his Jeffersonian art in the management of men. He was too much the psychologist arbitrarily to give orders. He was a genius in the art of suggestion. He had the subtlety to insinuate his own thoughts into the minds of his conferees, and he was a master in the art of permitting himself to be persuaded to the acceptance of his own ideas and plans. And along with these, he had other qualities, his adamantine honesty and a courage that never in the stormiest moments of his life flinched or faltered under fire.

But he had another implement in his armory that made him a powerful factor in the polemics of his time — a natural gift of eloquence that moved men to his will. He realized the concept of logic on fire, and there was grace and beauty in the flames. Out from a well-stored mind he spoke with a fluency that never faltered, for in his callow days in this very room, like Charles James Fox in the House of Commons, he had spoken with frequency in the perfecting of his art. He made his art so much an art that the artistry was not in evidence. Its cultivation was confined to the literary phrase, and he had trained his taste by constant communion with the greatest masters of poetry and prose. In delivery he had but to give nature rein, for nature had given him a dramatic sense, imagination, a capacity for righteous wrath, and a silvery voice that was an instrument of music.

Thus we had the motivating principles of his life; and the equipment with which, at the age of twenty-one, this young man, mature beyond his years, entered the House of Delegates, and sat within these walls. He entered when we were challenging the imperial power of England in the second war, and when the light from our burning Capitol illumined darkly the treason of the political foes of the Administration, Young Tyler's voice and vote were in support of Madison, and day by day his eloquence was heard urging a vigorous prosecution of the war. The revolutionary fire of his father tipped his tongue.

Here, too, he fought the battles of Jeffersonian democracy against the Bank, and laid down the principle in support of which in later life he was to rise to an heroic stature — that senators in a representative government are but the servants and never the sovereigns of the people they represent. Returned five times with practical unanimity, he was a veteran already at twenty-six when he was made a Member of the Executive Council and elected to the National House of Representatives.

Thus he entered the national arena a seasoned debater, a persuasive orator, his principles set in granite, and he moved with easy grace and with consent to a commanding position among his colleagues. Here, perhaps, that which was most significant of his prescience and genius as a leader, was his opposition to the Missouri Compromise. With Calhoun, that giant whose philosphic intellect has seldom been approached in all our history, supporting the measure, the voice of the Virginia youth of twenty-eight was courageously raised against it. And his, not Calhoun's, was the voice of prophecy. Now statesmanship is the gift of seeing into day after tomorrow. It was not the immediate purpose of the Compromise that he opposed; it was the accompanying concession of the constitutional right of Congress to legislate on slavery in the territories. Though not yet thirty, he foresaw what

[158]

others failed to see — that with the admission of the principle of congressional interference, the door was opened for the continuing agitation that ultimately would endanger the solidarity of the Union. He did not propose that the door should be opened with his consent; he raised his voice in prophetic warning, and hastening events would soon vindicate his judgment and prove his statesmanship.

With shattered health, he retired to private life at the age of thirty, only to be called by the mandate of the people at thirty-five to the gubernatorial honors of this historic Commonwealth; and brief though his tenure was, his instinct for constructive action served his people well. He found that the mountains raised a barrier between the people of the East and West; his was the dream to circumvent the mountains and thus make for the greater spiritual solidarity of Virginia. Under the pressure and inspiration of his leadership, the sections were closer knit by the canals and roads he built.

But to me, more important than his plan for the material improvement of Virginia, was his dream of extending the blessings of education to every son and daughter of the soil through the creation of a system of public schools. Jefferson, long before him, had had this dream and failed; and Tyler carried on, and failed; but it was from the seed sown and tended by the Jeffersons and Tylers that ultimately was to spring the great public school system of Virginia.

Thus when Tyler entered the Senate at the age of thirty-seven, he was definitely anchored to a political philosophy and adequately trained for statesmanship of a high order. It was the Senate's golden age, comparable to that of the British Parliament in the days of Pitt and Fox, of Burke and Sheridan, and destined to give to literature some of the greatest orations of all times, to engage in gladiatorial combats of the intellect never before approached on this side of the sea, and to deal with subjects that went to the very foundations of our governmental system. And into this glorious company, and into this portentous day stepped John Tyler, instantly to take high rank among the acknowledged leaders of that body.

Unhappily, we can only sketchily survey the part he played, and touch upon the more significant events. With economic issues and the slavery agitation driving a wedge between the sections, the sensitive political consciousness of Tyler caught, afar off, the ominous footbeats of marching men. He loved Virginia; his forbears from the days of the cavalier had helped direct its destiny and men of his blood were sleeping in its soil; but no man ever loved the Union conceived by the fathers more tenderly or truly. No statesman of his time dedicated his genius for conciliation more completely to the reconcilement of the sections through the healing processes of the legislation of compromise.

Scarcely had he taken his seat when the abominable tariff act of 1828 was forced upon the statutes. It was a tax on the agriculturists of the South to increase the profits of the industrialists of the North through the violation of economic laws. Even then, though few knew it, the irrepressible conflict was at hand. In his rural home at the foot of the Blue Ridge, Calhoun was meditating his doctrine of nullification. The sizzling pens of the Rhetts were preaching resistance in the press. To paraphrase Lord Churchill's famous sentence, hot-headed devotees of southern interest, giving more heat than light, were crying that "South Carolina will fight and South Carolina will be right." Emissaries of that great commonwealth were traversing the South seeking coöperation in resistance;

youth was toying nervously with its muskets; secret agents of the grim old man in the White House were beating a pathway to and from his door; and then — the Nullification Proclamation; and then — the Force bill.

Tyler had met the danger on the threshold and had fought the tariff of 1828 with all his zeal. He saw beyond the economic issue to the danger to the Union. The wisest, soundest, most prophetic speech against that measure of iniquity was that of Tyler; and Madison and John Marshall, divided in political affiliation, joined in lavish praise of the tone, the temper, and the content of the Tyler speech. You will search the records of the Congress in vain for a more persuasive and pathetic appeal to the better angels of our nature. Others were combatants in the fight; almost alone, John Tyler pled for peace through justice. But the bill was passed, and the storm clouds gathered, and there were rumblings on the far horizon; and then Nullification — and the Force bill.

Now John Tyler had no sympathy with nullification. "Let government be just," he said, "and nullification has no food on which to exist." But he had no sympathy with the Force bill. "It sweeps away," he said, "all the barriers of the Constitution." He had no faith in the unselfish patriotism of the beneficiaries of the tariff act. "The manufacturers will fight," he said, "rather than resign their profits."

And then, in the midst of the preparation for armed action, there came a pause. When at the instance of Virginia, South Carolina suspended the operation of her nullification act to give time for mediation, John Tyler stepped into the breach. Quietly he set about his task. The material was all before him. Here was the Force bill which ultimately meant war; here was nullification which meant the Force bill; and here was the tariff that meant nullification. Reduce the tariff, and nullification would die out, and the Force bill could be abandoned.

He looked about the Chamber for the human elements with which he had to work. There was Henry Clay whose autocratic and domineering ways had done so much to force the tariff act upon the statutes; and there was Calhoun, whose extreme opposition had brought the crisis on. Could these two men be brought together in a spirit of conciliation, by appeals to their patriotism, the situation might be saved. Already in a speech, Tyler had outlined the basis of a compromise. He proposed that if the manufacturers would agree to reduce the tariff to a revenue basis, there should be a gradual reduction to prevent the disorganization of their industries. That *was* the Compromise of 1833, and John Tyler was its father.

But would Clay agree to the reduction — or Calhoun consent to the delay? Tyler turned to them — these men who momentarily were not on speaking terms. Clay quailed a moment at the anticipated fury of the manufacturers, but only for a moment. How simply Tyler has told the story: "I appealed to his patriotism. No one ever did so in vain." And then, it was Tyler who persuaded Clay and Calhoun to a meeting. And with what Spartan brevity does he record the event, "They met, consulted, agreed."

And thus it was, when the very foundations of the Union shook, that Henry Clay arose to offer as the compromise of 1833 the very proposition Tyler previously had urged upon the Senate floor. The scene deserves the memorialization of a canvas. As Clay announced the compromise, he turned toward Tyler, and meeting in mid chamber, the two men clasped hands.

These two men were soon to become inveterate foes; and Tyler was to suffer through the other's acts. But in the twilight of his days, when Clay was dead, and in this city a monument to his memory was raised, John Tyler journeyed hither to pay tribute to his foe, to recall the scene that day in the Senate Chamber, and to say, "It is the clasp of that hand that has brought me here today." I know of nothing finer or nobler in the story of American politics. It mattered not to Tyler that his, the essential part, had been ignored by history, that all the credit might go to Clay. He was big enough to —

"*Take the cash and let the credit go
Nor heed the rumble of a distant drum.*"

It was enough for him that in a grave crisis in his country's history he had stepped into the breach when others faltered, and given the Union a new lease on life.

This was the supreme service of his senatorial career, but nothing in that career became him better than his manner of leaving it. He had fought for Jackson against the re-chartering of the National Bank; for Jackson's fight was in accordance with the fundamentals of his faith. He broke with Jackson on the removal of the deposits — and this was consistent with that faith as well. He conceived the removal an act of executive usurpation creating a precedent for a dangerous concentration of power, and he voted to spread a censure of the act upon the record. And when Virginia instructed him to vote to expunge the censure, he rose to heroic heights of manhood.

Throughout his life he had committed himself to the right of a constituency to instruct a representative, and now that principle pressed upon him. He did not hesitate. The people he represented had instructed him to vote against the dictates of his conscience. He *could* not vote against his conscience; he *would* not act against the instructions of his people; and thus, putting aside the cynical importunities of partisans, and scorning recourse to the sophistries of self-deception, he tendered his resignation, and filed out of the Senate Chamber in the proud company of his self-respect. I know of nothing so Cato-like in the austerity of its integrity as this act which gave new dignity to public station. The situation he confronted was the acid test of true greatness of mind and soul and John Tyler stood the test.

The four years that intervened between his resignation and his return to the national arena were crowded with political events. The Whigs, with whom he was affiliated, were maneuvering for position. The seed of disintegration was in that party's cradle, for it was an incongruous combination of inconsistent and utterly irreconcilable elements. And as the vice-presidential nominee of this hodge-podge party, John Tyler was elected in 1840, and almost immediately reached the Presidency through the death of Harrison.

Partisan historians have accused the Tyler of the Presidency with disloyalty to the Whigs — and this is false. He had made no compromise with his conscience for the nomination. He had yielded not one jot of his opposition to the protective tariff policy; and in the very heat of the campaign he had reiterated his uncompromising hostility to the National Bank. And did the Whigs then repudiate his leadership? No — they acclaimed his policy the platform of the party on which they appealed to the electorate of the Nation. Throughout the campaign of 1840, not one Whig statesman proposed the abandonment of the tariff compromise of 1833 ; not one Whig leader so much as hinted of a plan for the restoration of the Bank.

Ah, but do they say that there was no positive declaration to the contrary? The records are against them. Throughout the campaign the Whig press insisted with reiterated emphasis that the tariff and the Bank were no longer issues — that they were dead. The Whigs of the Legislature of Virginia formally proclaimed the promise and the pledge that their victory at the polls would not be followed by an attempt to increase the tariff or to recharter the bank. The Whig campaign was made upon the principles of John Tyler as its platform; and had the party deviated one hair's breadth from him on fundamental principles, he would have flung the nomination back into its lap.

And now the victory is won — and now Harrison, with the laurel wreath of triumph fresh upon him, lies in the White House, dead; and now John Tyler succeeds to the Presidency. Now the Whigs, with a brazen effrontery, unparalleled in American history, throw off the mask of hypocrisy and prepare to push the very policies they themselves renounced when seeking the suffrage of the people — and now John Tyler confronts them and dismays them with the spectacle of an honest statesman who refuses to be a party to the intolerable treachery.

Picture to yourself the isolation of his position. He had incurred the hostility of the Democrats by his opposition to Jackson; and he challenges now the hatred of the Whigs by his fidelity to the pledge and principles on which he was elected.

The first to reach the Presidency through succession, they seek to minimize his power and belittle his position; and by meeting them with a stern and dignified assertion of his constitutional status he rendered an immeasurable service to the republic.

But meanwhile, with much waving of banners, his party is moving toward the deliberate betrayal of its pledge under the hypnotic influence of the incomparable Clay. Thus Tyler received his ultimatum — the surrender of his principles or the repudiation of his party. Conscious of

the seriousness of the situation, he moved with a statesman's instinct for reasonable conciliation, and proposed
a compromise consistent with his constitutional objections
to the bank, the establishment of a District Bank in
Washington with branches in the States, provided the
States gave consent. It was a statesman's proffer of peace;
and brushing it aside, Clay sought the creation of another
bank like that which the people, with reason, had destroyed. Then it was, that John Tyler proved his mettle
by meeting the impudent betrayal with a vigorous veto,
and Clay turned loose upon him the dogs of war. In Whig
communities he was burned in effigy, and even threatened
with assassination.

Before the storm fanned by the bellows of the repudiated
bank, John Tyler stood erect, serene in the consciousness
of duty done; and when another bank bill equally offensive
was enacted, he killed it with a veto once again. The
Cabinet, bowing to the will of Clay, filed out; all but
Webster, who refused to stoop.

Once more Tyler concentrated his constructive mind upon
finance, and eventually evolved his Exchequer System, pronounced by Webster at Faneuil Hall, " the most beneficial
institution, the Constitution alone excepted " to the credit
of American statesmanship. But partisanship prevailed;
the Whigs refused the measure; and thus through the
remainder of his Administration, John Tyler was the
custodian of the Nation's money, and in the end he turned
it over without the misplacement of a single cent. The
record of Tyler on finance was that of honesty and political
integrity, of constructive capacity and conciliation, as
far as honor went; it was as a shaft of wholesome light
in a darkened room.

Again they tested his honor with a tariff measure ob-
noxious to his conscience and they met his instant veto with

personal abuse and the menace of impeachment; and he stood in the storm again unbowed, serene, and in the end prevailed. To find another President as dignified and unswerving in the face of foul abuse, one must come down to the days of Andrew Johnson.

But not always did partisanship and faction intervene to thwart him in his domestic policies; and, free from that, his record as administrator was one of quick decision, forceful action, and a conciliating tact. Thus he turned to the Seminole war in Florida that seven years of fighting had failed to end; he ended it with victory in a few scant months and the red men moved toward the sunset and the white settlers moved in to redeem the waste places to the purposes of men. Thus he faced the unprecedented challenge of the Dorr Rebellion in Rhode Island; and it dissipated before the disclosure of his clear intent to put down insurrection, even though the men in arms were demanding what he himself conceived to be their inalienable rights. He put the insurrection down without the firing of a shot, without the movement of a soldier, without inflicting a solitary wound to the principle of State Rights. Unhampered by factious opposition, he met every domestic issue with rare executive ability.

But even so the prospect brightens when we turn to international affairs. In his contacts with the diplomatic corps he was singularly happy; for his elegance of manner, his suavity, and old-world courtesy gave a charm to his diplomatic conversations. He was by nature a conciliator. He had a genius for negotiations. He had the power, no matter how hot his blood, of keeping his head cool. And seldom had such qualities been so imperatively needed as when he entered upon his Presidency. The clouds on the international horizon were low and threatening and our relations with England were dangerously impaired. The controversy over the northern boundary, continuing through six administrations, had finally found Maine and New Brunswick facing each other, armed, across the border. The incident of the *Caroline* was pressing for solution, and diplomacy had reached an impasse; and the arrest of a British subject for murder in that connection was threatening to break the diplomatic relations of the English-speaking nations. The searching of American vessels by British cruisers, under the pretext of suppressing the slave trade, had brought on an acrimonious debate. It was under these delicate conditions that Lord Ashburton, a bluff and honest Britisher, sacrificed the serenity of his retirement from public life, at the summons of patriotism and humanity, to undertake, in Washington, the negotiation of a general treaty of amity. No finer figure has appeared in such a cause upon our shores.

We cannot enter into the details of the famous Webster-Ashburton treaty. Suffice it to say that it measurably succeeded in the settlement of all disputes and probably prevented another war. We know the story of the negotiations over the wine and walnuts in the exchange of dinners between Webster and Ashburton in the houses in LaFayette Square; we know the difficulties that constantly threatened rupture; we know that in the deadly miasmic heat of a Washington summer, the negotiators, frequently on edge, and worn to utter exhaustion, were more than once upon the point of breaking off. All honor to the part then played by Daniel Webster, but it was John Tyler who saved the situation more than once by his persuasive tact. Throughout the negotiations he seemingly stood aloof, confiding in his minister, but not a move was made by Webster without a consultation with his chief. His was the decisive voice in every instance. It was in the conferences of that summer's heat that these two

[168]

men acquired that admiration for each other's qualities which persisted through their lives.

One scene from the drama of those negotiations — one not dissimilar to others. In the determination of the boundary line the two ministers have apparently reached the end of their concessions. The accumulating irritations of the prolonged debate have seemingly made the prospects hopeless. The negotiators are sulking in their tents. The aged Ashburton, sweltering and sickening in the unaccustomed humidity and heat, is ready to abandon further efforts and return to England.

And now John Tyler steps into the breach. He invites the British diplomat to a conversation. Instead of the scowling, fighting face of the irritated Webster, he looks into the serene and sympathetic countenance of Tyler. The atmosphere of controversy is missing now. Nowhere about is to be seen the paraphernalia of combat. And he listens to a kindly, soothing human being making a moving human appeal. He hears an appeal that ignores diplomacy and goes directly to the heart of the generous old man who required no sensational diplomatic triumph to serve the purposes of personal ambition. He hears a reminder that upon the amicable solution of the pressing problems may rest the peace of people bound together by a common language, a common literature, and common traditions of freedom. And he hears the direct appeal to him, "If you cannot settle them, what man in England can?" Before that tactful and almost tender appeal the old man melts. "Well, well, Mr. President," he splutters, "well, well, we must try again." One need not detract one iota from the claims of the two negotiators to conclude that but for the conciliatory genius, the calming serenity, and the pervasive humanity of John Tyler these negotiations might have failed and war have come.

[169]

The foreign policy of John Tyler was strong as dignity, and conciliatory as humanity. He erased from the agenda of controversy some of the most complicated problems of his time. He had strength without bluster, firmness without stubbornness, and patriotism without chauvinism. History has conceded his triumphs in the field of international relations. The same qualities that made him the conciliator of the Senate made him the peace-maker of the English-speaking peoples at a critical period of their relations.

And now we reach the supreme triumph of his administration. For many years the most prescient statesmen had foreseen the need of the imperial territory of Texas properly to round out the Nation's destiny. Adams had bartered for it and failed. Jackson had increased the offer many fold and failed. Meanwhile the hardy race of American pioneers in Texas had risen in revolt, and on the bloody field of San Jacinto successfully had challenged the authority of Mexico, and proclaimed their independence. With its charter of independence in its hand, signed by the nations of the world, it had offered annexation to Van Buren who preferred to await the proof of its ability to withstand the assault of Mexico. Five years of testing had intervened before the Presidency of John Tyler, and despite sporadic dashes of outlaws from across the border to plunder, to murder, and to burn, there stood Texas, unshaken and unshakable in her independence, a sovereign nation, master of her destiny.

Within six months of his accession John Tyler planned to make the acquisition of Texas a major accomplishment of his Administration. He saw in Texas the rounding out of our national destiny; he saw an empire of immeasurable potentialities in wealth and power eager for annexation; and, noting her struggles against marauders, her credit failing, he foresaw the danger of intrigue from England or from France. Within six months he had urged the project of annexation by treaty upon Webster in an historic letter. But conditions were not then ripe. The minister of Texas was in our capital pleading for annexation; but we had private claims pending against the government of Mexico, and we had to wait on that. There were factions in the Senate which would pass upon the treaty, and the unification of these forces had to be managed with *finesse;* and we had to wait on that. And while we waited, England, with fifty millions loaned in Mexico, was casting a threatening shadow on the scene; for when we seemed to spurn the Texas plea to take an empire for the asking, she turned a receptive ear to the whisperings of the diplomacy of Britain. The abolitionists were on the war path now, and soon Lord Brougham, thundering in parliament against slavery, would be expatiating glowingly upon the material advantages of the rich domain. The hour had struck for action; delay was dangerous.

Webster had now departed, and Tyler instructed Upshur, his successor, to offer a treaty of annexation to the Texan Minister under the seal of secrecy. It was none too soon. Already Houston, the Texas President, was under the spell of England, and Texas was involved in the intrigue. Already the hardy American pioneers in Texas, in ignorance of the maneuvering behind the scenes, and discouraged by our seeming indifference to the plea for annexation, were despairing of relief from us; and then, just then, a ringing message to the Congress from John Tyler, denouncing the Mexican intermeddling in Texas and demanding that it cease. The people of Texas heard, and understood, and cheered; the British intrigue was underminded and wrecked.

Meanwhile Ulshur was canvassing the Senate for a

constitutional majority for the treaty; finding ways he hoped would prevent the raising of a party issue; drawing men together on the higher grounds of patriotism. And out from his seclusion at the Hermitage, Andrew Jackson stepped to the side of Tyler; the Jacksonians fell in line behind their leader; and as Frémont, the son-in-law of Benton, turned with the President's commission toward the Oregon trail, Old Bullion whirled into the Administration camp on Texas. And then tragedy intervened with the death of Upshur.

Out from his retirement at the foot of the Blue Ridge, Calhoun, now, with some misgivings, was summoned to the portfolio of State. Under the once prevalent, and now discredited abolitionist misinterpretation of history, Calhoun was credited with the move for Texas. Absurd assumption! The treaty was completed before Calhoun took office; the negotiations were over; and he was to contribute nothing of material importance. He had opposed the pressing of the project in a letter still preserved in the archives of the State Department; and after the event was consummated he frankly avowed his remonstrance at the time in a public speech.

It was Tyler who led and dictated at every single step. It was he who first raised the issue in his letter to Webster; it was he who ordered Upshur to proceed; and the project was completed and the treaty framed before Calhoun took over the portfolio of State.

And now England has been thwarted, Texas has been conciliated, the treaty has been completed, and transmitted to the Senate with a stirring message. And now Henry Clay appears to evoke the specter of party to defeat it, and Van Buren declares against it, and the abolitionists denounce it; and under the lashings of the whip of Clay, and through the contriving of Van Buren, enough Senators are persuaded to the repudiation of their pledge to defeat the ratification. America, through political perfidy and personal ambitions, had refused an empire as a gift.

But John Tyler had only begun to fight. The campaign of 1844 was on. With Clay and Polk contending for the Presidency, and neither standing for immediate annexation, John Tyler accepted an independent nomination — and unfurled the flag of Texas. With the certainty that the persistence of his candidacy would sound the knell of Polk, he met the importunities to withdraw with the dictation of his terms. If Polk and the Democrats would take the banner of Texas from his hands and bear it openly into the fight, and keep the faith, he would retire. The pledge was made, the pledge was kept, and thus the treaty was ratified in the closing hours of Tyler's administration, and the annexation of Texas was an accomplished fact. Thus the monument to the administration of Tyler is a vast empire brought beneath the flag — Texas is his monument!

When he laid down the burdens of the Presidency, John Tyler could review it with pride in his achievements and in the fidelity with which he had clung to all the fundamentals of his faith. The astonishing vulgarity of his foes had not even tempted him to part company with his gentility. If he had broken with his party, it was because his party had chosen the path of perfidy and dishonor. He had kept faith with the people, and his manly vetoes of every act of treachery compels history's tribute to his impeccable personal and political integrity. He had created precedents and made the policies of a people; had defined and enforced the constitutional status of a President succeeding through the death of a predecessor; had met his constitutional obligations in the Dorr rebellion with meticulous respect for the sovereign rights of States; had adopted the formula of annexation through the treaty, which McKinley was to follow. He broke new ground, and in every instance the furrow that he plowed has become the fixed landmark of the Republic. He had found our international problems pressing, and with finesse had solved them; and, dissipating by diplomacy and determination the intrigues that intervened, had brought a great empire of untold value under the jurisdiction of the flag and forever associated with the Lone Star State the name of Tyler.

I know of nothing in our history more dignified or scrupulously correct than the character of John Tyler's retirement to Sherwood Forest. Even there he guarded the dignity of the Presidency with a cautious reticence. He followed with patriotic interest the course of public affairs, but no merely captious criticism from him embarrassed his successors. In the serenity of his retreat he turned again to the beloved classics of English literature from Addison and Steele, from Milton and Shakespeare to Macaulay, and in that goodly company forgot the provocative and futile wranglings of lesser men. Now and then, we see him emerging from his retirement to deliver special occasion orations that are contributions to history. To me the retired statesman of Sherwood Forest was not unlike the Sir William Temple of Moor Park in his cloistered aloofness; but that "pale" patriotism that Macaulay found in Temple he did not share. From the watch tower of his country home, he had a more perfect perspective on moving events than those who were participating, and he watched with grave concern the gathering of the forces that were threatening the perpetuity of our institutions. He stood four square for the compromises of the Constitution, and for the preservation of the Union of the fathers. With reservations, he hailed the compromise of 1850 as a possible harbinger of peace.

But passions and sordid economic interests were in the saddle and riding hard — and riding down the better instincts of our nature. A course and brutal prophet of the new day dawning was lightly saying that a little blood letting would do us good. Sectionalism mobilized in parties and was ready for the fray. The crisis came, proclaimed in raucous accents; and then it was that an old man who had sat at the feet of the sage of Monticello, emerged from his retirement in Sherwood Forest to seek another compromise to save the Nation from internecine strife. What a picture — This of an old man turning away from the delights of his library and the joys of domesticity to spend his waning strength in the cause of peace!

Thus in the midst of the tumult and the shouting is heard again the calm conciliating voice of John Tyler. The statesman, surrounded by a jostling mob of politicians, has evolved a plan. He knows, or thinks, that the one remaining hope of a compromise of peace lies in the conservatism of the border States, and he urges a convention of these Commonwealths. "These," he writes, "are the most interested in keeping peace, and if they cannot come to an understanding, then the political Union is gone, as is already, to a great extent, the union of fraternal feeling. "Had his plan been taken, without deviation, there might have been some hope; but when the call included all the States that hope was blasted.

And now the venerable statesman of Sherwood Forest is summoned to service once again. The problem of the moment is to prevent an act of violence from breaking in upon the processes of conciliation. As Virginia dispatches an emissary to South Carolina, John Tyler hastens to that other venerable patriot, President Buchanan. Again Tyler enters the White House, where Dolly Madison had first received him, to plead for peace and Union. We

[175]

see Buchanan yielding to his persuasive plea and importuning Congress against hostile legislation for the moment. We see Stanton acting as his messenger as he seeks to prevent the premature movement of troops. An old man, pleading for moderation and conciliation as the storm came on! We see him, a little later, presiding over the Peace Convention, and hear his beautifully moving appeal to the common memories and nobler sentiments of our people. We see him introducing the members of the Convention to Abraham Lincoln; and, returning the call, we see the gaunt figure of the President-elect enter the parlor of John Tyler. All that a man could do for peace and Union, this unselfish patriot then did; but the dogs of war were straining at their leashes, and the voice of conciliation could not be heard above the dreadful din.

And thus John Tyler carries home the consciousness of failure, consoled by the reflection that he, at least, had done his part. We hear him in the Virginia convention confess his failure with the pathetic comment that he had hoped for a success that would be the "proud crowning" of his life.

And now the conflict he had sought to check throughout his life comes on; and John Tyler casts his lot with the people of Virginia, the home of his fathers, whose ashes mingled with her soil. His voice was not to be heard in the Confederate Congress, where he accepted service. Just as the thunder of the guns began, his spirit winged its way "beyond the sunset and the stars." Happily for him, he was spared the pathos of the bloody struggle, and the intolerable persecution of his people that followed, like vultures, in the wake of war.

Such is the story of the man whose bust we unveil today.

" Statesman, yet friend to truth, of soul sincere,
In action faithful, and in honor clear."

[176]

His public life had been based upon the fundamental principles of Jefferson and from these he never deviated one hair's breadth that "thrift might follow fawning." In the Plutarch of our Republic one will look in vain for a public figure of greater courage, of more impeccable integrity; for a stouter champion of liberty and the rights of man; for one more unselfish in the service of the state; or one inspired by a purer patriotism. Here in the classic building that Jefferson designed, in this room hallowed by heroic memories, we place his bust with those of others whom Virginia has given to the nation and mankind, that future generations passing through may look upon the features of — a Man.

ZACHARY TAYLOR

President of the United States
1849–1850

Brigadier-General JOHN A. LEJEUNE, The Speaker

FROM THE INTRODUCTION OF THE SPEAKER

by

GOVERNOR POLLARD

On the immortal roll of American Presidents will be found the names of many military leaders. History shows that our people delight to honor in time of peace those who have fought our battles in time of war — Washington, Jackson, Harrison, Taylor, and Grant were all great warriors but all of them joined Washington in the prayer that the plague of war might be banished from the earth. War with all its horrors, its sufferings, and its tears has its roots in mistakes made in time of peace. All of these soldier Presidents had a burning desire that their country avoid the mistakes which lead to war.

On this occasion of the unveiling of this bust, I count ourselves fortunate that the tribute to a hero of the Mexican War should be paid by a hero of the World War. He comes from the State of Louisiana where Zachary Taylor spent much of his life. Taylor, born in Virginia, went to Louisiana. Lejeune, born in Louisiana,

F. WILLIAM SIEVERS, *The Sculptor*

distinguished in the World War, comes to Virginia to lend his name, his fame, and his magnificent talents to the upbuilding of the Virginia Military Institute. As I present him to this audience, may I take occasion to acknowledge the joy of our people that he has come to live and labor among us.

On behalf of the Commonwealth of Virginia I accept from Mr. Jaquelin P. Taylor of Orange County, Virginia, a kinsman of President Taylor, the gift of this beautiful bust of Zachary Taylor. I extend to the generous donor the sincere thanks of the people of this State.

JAQUELIN P. TAYLOR, *The Donor*

Mr. F. William Sievers, the sculptor, has well produced in marble the strength as well as the kindliness of the countenance of the warrior and statesman we honor today. Virginia is proud to have living within her borders a sculptor whose genius is recognized throughout the country.

ZACHARY TAYLOR

ADDRESS BY

Brigadier-General JOHN A. LEJEUNE

I AM very grateful to Governor Pollard for having done me the honor of selecting me to deliver the address on the occasion of the unveiling of the bust of one of the eight Presidents of the United States who were born in the State of Virginia; and, for a number of reasons, I am especially grateful for the fact that to me has come the distinction of being chosen to discuss the career and the character of President Zachary Taylor.

While Zachary Taylor was born in the State of Virginia, he established his residence in the State of Louisiana and became a citizen of that State towards the close of his long service as an officer of the regular Army. The speaker, on the other hand, was born in the State of Louisiana and has established his residence in the State of Virginia and has become a citizen of that State towards the close of his long service — forty-seven years — as an officer of the regular Marine Corps. Perhaps the Governor's knowledge of this fact may, at least, partly explain some of the motives which actuated him in selecting the speaker for this pleasing though difficult task.

My old home was not far from the Louisiana home of General Taylor, and as a boy, I distinctly remember the affection with which he was regarded by the older men of my family and of neighboring families who had known him during his residence in Louisiana or during the Mexican War.

One of my earliest memories is his picture which in 1849 my father had placed in the glass door which protected the works and the pendulum of the old mantel clock which ticked away the hours in our home during the seventeen years that I lived there before I entered the United States Naval Academy and the Naval Service and began my wanderings over the face of the earth.

Among our near neighbors, too, was a family of Taylors who were closely related to General Taylor, and I cherish as one of my choicest possessions a beautiful silver goblet which the head of that family presented to my great Uncle Dr. John G. Archer as a token of his gratitude for his skillful and successful treatment of a faithful male servant a few years before the Civil war. The goblet, many years afterwards, was given to me by Dr. Archer's widow for the reason that I was named for him at my birth.

I find, too, that President Taylor had some interesting contacts with the Virginia Military Institute. On February 22, 1850, he visited the city of Richmond for the purpose of participating in the corner-stone laying, at the Capitol, of the statue of the great man who was the first President of the United States, and the Corps of Cadets acted as his body guard while in Richmond, and was reviewed by him after the conclusion of the ceremonies. President Taylor, in token of the admiration with which he regarded the Cadets, directed the War Department to present to the Corps the four light bronze cannon with which the Cadet battery of artillery was armed and with which it drilled under the watchful eye and the stern discipline of the officer who, in the crucial days of the War between the States, immortalized himself under the name of Stonewall Jackson. These same guns after effective service with Jackson, in that heroic struggle, notably at the Battle of Bull Run in June, 1861, and after many years' active use at the Institute subsequent to that War, are now parked in front of the Cadet Barracks, where they stand silent and peaceful guard over the bronze statue of the remarkable military genius to whom I have just referred and whose deeds brought undying fame to Virginia, to the Confederacy, and to America.

* *
*

To take up the thread of my narrative, I must needs turn from the present to the long-distant past or to November, 1784, to be more exact, when the babe Zachary Taylor first saw the light of day in the farmhouse home of his father and mother in Orange County, Virginia.

His father, Colonel Richard Taylor, served throughout the War of the Revolution with distinction. He was a personal friend of General Washington, a near relative of President James Madison, and was connected with many of the historic Virginia families, such as the Lees, the Marshalls, and the Taliaferros. His wife, formerly Miss Strother, was a charming Virginia lady whose beautiful character left an impress on all who knew her.

Colonel "Dick" Taylor, Zachary's father, was from boyhood filled with the spirit of adventure which caused him in his early youth to join a party of explorers on a voyage down the Ohio and Mississippi rivers as far as Natchez, from which place he returned to his Virginia home on foot and alone. It is not surprising, therefore, that his thoughts, like those of many other veterans of the War of the Revolution, should have turned towards the West, or that in 1785, when his son, Zachary, was less than a year old, he and his family should have moved to Kentucky, the then frontier, where they established themselves neaɪ the present city of Louisville, on land which they cleared and cultivated and on which they built their home.

That part of Kentucky was then a wild country inhabited by savages, and young Zachary spent his most impressionable years in an atmosphere of strife. Warfare between the Indians and the settlers was the normal state of existence then, and the boys were taught the use of weapons and the strategem of combat even before they learned to read or to cipher.

Young Zachary received instruction in the rudiments of book learning from his mother, and, also, had the benefit of some schooling under the tutelage of Mr. Ayres, a Connecticut schoolmaster, who was engaged by Colonel Taylor and a few neighbors as the tutor of their boys.

His education, a meager one, was supplemented by the careful reading of good books, a practice which he followed, diligently, throughout his life time, so that like Lincoln, and thousands of other pioneers, he was, chiefly, a self-educated man.

Although he was brought up to be a farmer, his tastes lay in the direction of a military life ; but he became reconciled to following the more humdrum career, owing to the seeming impossibility of obtaining a commission, the family influence having been exhausted when his older brother was appointed a Lieutenant in the then very small regular Army.

On the unexpected death of that brother, in 1808, however, young Zachary, through the personal interest in him of Mr. James Madison, was commissioned by President Jefferson to fill the vacancy in the Seventh Infantry which was caused by his brother's death.

His two-years service as a Lieutenant was of a routine nature, consisting of garrison duty in New Orleans, where he contracted the yellow fever, and in the small posts which dotted the frontier. In 1810, he received his promotion to the rank of Captain, a few months after his marriage to Miss Margaret Smith of Calvert County, Maryland. History and tradition alike ascribe to her not only much charm and grace of manner but the more substantial virtues as well. Unquestionably, she was a lovely, industrious, home-loving, Christian gentlewoman, and as is the case with good wives did much to advance the interests of her husband and to influence beneficently the lives of their children, one of whom became Mrs. Jefferson Davis, another General "Dick" Taylor, a famous Confederate, and still another the wife of Colonel Bliss of the Army, a trusted assistant and adviser of the General in Mexico and of the President in Washington.

In 1811, Captain Taylor's Regiment was transferred to the Northwestern Territory of which General William Henry Harrison was the Military Governor. It was in that theater of operations that Captain Taylor served throughout the War of 1812, and it was there that he participated actively in the campaigns against the Indian tribes which were in alliance with the British.

It was in one of those campaigns that he first distinguished himself by his heroic and successful defense of a small isolated fort near Vincennes, Indiana, against determined attacks by several hundred Indians. The small garrison except ten or twelve men was physically disabled by a virulent form of malarial fever with which they had been stricken; but it, nevertheless, succeeded, under Captain Taylor's inspiring leadership, in extinguishing a fire in one of the buildings which the Indians had started, and in repulsing their frequent attacks which continued throughout the night. In recognition of the courage and efficiency he displayed, he was promoted to the rank of

Major by brevet, the first commission of the kind issued by the United States War Department.

Following the War of 1812, he was advanced step by step to the rank of Colonel, attaining that grade in 1832. In the intervening years, practically all of his service was on the frontier where he was in contact with the Indians and the pioneer settlers. It was an inconspicuous but most useful service, involving as it did the maintenance of friendly relations with the aborigines by not only exhibiting towards them the qualities of firmness, justness, and kindliness, which were his dominant traits, but also, when necessity so required, by engaging in determined and persistent military reprisals, which had successful terminations in spite of the natural difficulties encountered in the wilderness and in spite of the treachery, the cunning, and the courage displayed by the savage foe.

Such distinction as he had gained was, in all probability, known only to the Indians, the frontiersmen, and the Army, as it is doubtful if the civilian population of the Eastern seaboard States had any knowledge of his record or had even heard his name mentioned prior to 1837, when it was announced that Colonel Zachary Taylor had been selected by the War Department to command the field forces in the military operations to be again undertaken against the Seminole Indians in Florida.

These Indians, under the leadership of their redoubtable Chief, Osceola, had, hitherto, been successful in eluding the columns which were sent in pursuit of them, and in making surprise attacks on small isolated detachments. In addition, they had harried the countryside, burned farmhouses, driven off cattle, and massacred the scattered settlers.

In fact the so-called Seminole War had dragged along for a number of years without a decisive result. Finally, the War Department turned to Colonel Taylor, an officer who enjoyed among his brother officers of the Army the reputation of possessing, in an unusual degree, the qualities of common sense and indomitable will combined with experience in savage warfare which were so essential to success in a theater of operations like that of southern Florida and against an astute and wily leader like the Seminole Chief.

Suffice it to relate that in a single campaign which involved great hardship and many almost insuperable difficulties, and which terminated in the decisive defeat of Osceola and his followers at the battle of Okeechobee, Colonel Taylor so shattered the morale of the Seminoles that the relentless minor operations which he at once instituted eventually brought about the surrender of the hostiles and their removal to the West.

Colonel Taylor was promoted to the rank of Brigadier General by brevet in recognition of his distinguished services in the battle of Okeechobee, and in 1840, he was transferred to the command of the Southwestern Department with Headquarters at Baton Rouge, and at Fort Jessup, Louisiana.

The Southwestern Department embraced the States of Alabama, Mississippi, Arkansas, and Louisiana, and was, therefore, contiguous to the Republic of Texas, which had recently been able to separate itself from Mexico after a sanguinary struggle, and which was then an applicant for admission as one of the United States of America.

The proposed admission of Texas into the Union was a burning political question for several years. Henry Clay, the leader of the Whig party, was on the side of the opposition, and upon his nomination in 1844 as the Whig candidate for President, he fought the campaign on that issue. He was defeated, however, by James K. Polk of Tennessee, the candidate of the Democratic Party.

General Taylor, although a Whig, took no part in the controversy, but like the fine old soldier he was, stood in readiness to carry out loyally and faithfully the instructions of the Commander-in-Chief without regard to which party he belonged and without regard to the political policy involved.

Early in March, 1845, Congress passed the Enabling Act with reference to Texas, and in July of that year, the Independent Republic of Texas accepted the terms of the act, and became one of the States of the Union, as soon as the necessary formalities were complied with.

Inasmuch as the Mexican Government bitterly resented the annexation by the United States of one of its former provinces, the independence of which it had never recognized, it was manifestly wise for the United States Government to provide the newly acquired State with military protection. This it proceeded to do in July, 1845, when General Taylor was directed to move his available forces by sea from New Orleans to Aransas Bay, Texas.

On July 25, he landed on St. Joseph Island with the advanced guard of his Expeditionary Force; and, in the course of about three weeks, he established and occupied a camp at Corpus Christi, near the mouth of the Nueces River. At Corpus Christi his force was gradually reënforced until it reached what was then regarded as the respectable number of three thousand nine hundred officers and men — a few more than a full-strength Regiment of the World War. This force, however, was formidably organized, being divided into three Infantry Brigades, a Regiment of Dragoons, several batteries of regular and New Orleans Artillery, and a detachment of the Texas Rangers.

The controversy with Mexico involved not only the annexation of Texas but likewise a dispute over the southern boundary of that State which the United States Government rightfully insisted was the Rio Grande. On January 13, 1846, immediately after the receipt of official dispatches indicating the adoption of a bellicose attitude by Mexico, the War Department directed General Taylor to march his force from Corpus Christi to the Rio Grande and to establish his camp on the north bank of that river. He was cautioned at the same time not to regard Mexico as an enemy unless war were declared or unless that nation should open hostilities.

On the eighth of March, General Taylor began his advance of about two hundred miles, after notifying the Mexican Commander at Matamoras and the civil population of the disputed territory, that his intentions were pacific. He arrived at his destination on March 23, and pitched his main camp opposite to Matamoras. His supply base he established at Point Isabel, near the mouth of the Rio Grande, and he constructed a fort adjacent to his main camp, which was afterwards designated as Fort Brown, in honor of Major Brown, who was killed while defending it.

The relations between the Mexican and the United States forces were very strained from the beginning, but no overt act was committed, until General Arista, the Mexican Commander, directed the crossing of the Rio Grande by a Cavalry force of one thousand men under the command of General Torreón, which, on April 25, surprised, attacked, defeated, and captured a United States Cavalry reconnoitering patrol (sixty men), commanded by Major Thornton.

This engagement marked the beginning of the war. "Hostilities have begun," announced General Arista.

"Hostilities may now be considered as commenced," reported General Taylor on the twenty-sixth, and, at the same time, called on Texas and Louisiana for five thousand men as reënforcements, and advised the President to issue a call for volunteers. Unquestionably the war was initiated by Mexico. President Paredes wrote on April 18, 1846, to General Arista, the Mexican Commander at Matamoras, as follows: "It is indispensable that hostilities begin, yourself taking the initiative," and in December, 1847, General Arista, himself, declared, "I had the pleasure of being the first to begin the war."

General Taylor foresaw that an attempt would be made to sever his line of communications with his supply base, and to capture the small fort at Point Isabel which guarded it. He, therefore, on May 1, marched his main body towards that place, leaving at Fort Brown, as a garrison, the Seventh Infantry and two batteries of artillery. On the same day, General Arista, with his army of five or six thousand men, crossed to the north bank of the Rio Grande, laid seige to Fort Brown, and, with the main body of his force, took up a position at Palo Alto, between Fort Brown and General Taylor's Army.

After nearly a week spent in improving the fortifications of Point Isabel and in making preparations to conduct a large wagon train of supplies to Fort Brown, General Taylor started on his return march to Fort Brown, with a detachment of twenty-three hundred men, eight light field pieces, two eighteen pounders, and a train of three hundred wagons.

On the following afternoon, May 8, he made contact with the Mexican Army. An engagement, known in history as the battle of Palo Alto, ensued, in which the artillery played the leading rôle. It was fought by the Americans in the thick chapparal, against an enemy nearly thrice their strength. The firing ceased at dusk. The Americans bivouacked in line of battle in close proximity to the Mexicans. During the night, the Mexican Army fell back to La Resaca de la Palma.

A few hours after daylight, General Taylor resumed his advance. Early in the afternoon, he gained contact with General Arista's force, which occupied a strong defensive position. On his front was a shallow but rather wide ravine and on his flanks were difficult obstacles. General Taylor promptly deployed his infantry, brought up his artillery, and attacked the Mexican center. A bitter contest ensued in which two batteries of Mexican artillery (eight guns) were captured and which soon thereafter ended in the defeat of the Mexican force, which retreated from the field. The retreat soon became a disorderly rout, especially during the crossing to the south bank of the Rio Grande. Nearly two hundred Mexican dead and large quantities of supplies were left on the battlefield, and a number of prisoners were captured by the victorious Americans.

The city of Matamoras at once became untenable, and a few days later it was evacuated by General Arista, who, with his beaten and demoralized army, retired to Monterey, the capital city of Nuevo Leon Province. Matamoras was promptly occupied by the American forces without opposition, and passed for the period of the war under the control of the just and mild military government which was then established by General Taylor.

On May 12, the United States Congress adopted a resolution declaring that a state of war existed between the United States and Mexico, and that it had been caused by the hostile acts of the latter nation, and empowering the President to enroll fifty thousand volunteers in the army. It also promptly indicated its gratitude to the successful commander by authorizing the President to promote him to the rank of Major General.

General Taylor was anxious to follow up his successes by an immediate advance to Monterey, but was compelled to endure a delay of three months, owing to the lack of both land and river transportation, and to the necessity of equipping and training the volunteer recruits which streamed into his camp at Matamoras in comparatively large numbers.

In July, the advance guard moved by road towards Camargo, a small town about one hundred eighty miles farther up the Rio Grande, and, at the same time, the steamboats carrying supplies started on their long voyage up the crooked, shallow river. On August 4, General Taylor transferred his headquarters by boat from Matamoras to Camargo. At Camargo, he established his advanced supply base, and assembled his army, preliminary to moving against Monterey, about one hundred eighty miles to the southward.

At the end of August, the campaign was initiated by the advance of General Worth's division. It was followed some days later by General Twigg's division, while General Butler's division constituted the rear guard. The three columns were concentrated at Ceralvo, a small town lying at the base of the Sierra Madre Mountains and about sixty miles north of Monterey.

The army after a short rest resumed its march, and on September 19 went into camp in plain view of the city of Monterey. General Taylor's army at Monterey consisted of three thousand eighty regulars and three thousand one hundred fifty volunteers, or a total of six thousand two hundred thirty officers and men, supported by four light batteries, two twenty-four-pound howitzers, and one ten-inch mortar. The Mexican Army was of slightly greater strength, and possessed, in addition, the pronounced advantage of occupying a city of stone and brick houses which was defended by heavy guns mounted in well-placed forts.

A thorough reconnaissance of the enemy's position was made at once, and the plan of attack decided on as soon as the report of the reconnoitering patrols was made. The plan provided for a turning movement to the westward of the city in order to gain control of the highway to Saltillo, which constituted the Mexican line of communications and avenue of retreat, and a secondary or supporting attack to be directed against the forts guarding the approaches to the city from the East.

At noon, the next day — September 20 — the turning movement was initiated by General Worth's division. It completed its march by nightfall and attacked the western forts at dawn the ensuing day; at the same time the divisions of General Twiggs and General Butler advanced as planned.

An obstinate struggle of three days' duration ensued, in which General Worth's division successfully accomplished its mission, while the supporting attacks on the eastern front of the city gained a partial success at the expense of rather heavy casualties in the house-to-house fighting.

At daylight on September 24, General Ampudia, the Mexican Commander, proposed a temporary cessation of hostilities for the purpose of arranging for the surrender of the city. Several days were spent in negotiations, which finally resulted in an agreement providing for the evacuation of Monterey by the Mexican Army, its occupation by the American Army, and an armistice for a period of eight weeks.

The clause referring to the armistice was disapproved by

the President, and General Taylor, after notifying the Mexican Commander accordingly, resumed active operations on November 12 by the advance of General Worth's division to Saltillo, a march of about sixty-five miles to the southwest. Some weeks later, General Twiggs' Division occupied Victoria, where a junction was effected with General Patterson's column which had marched down the coast from Matamoras and with the American forces which had recently occupied Tampico with the coöperation of the United States Fleet.

It was at about that time that General Taylor received a letter from Major General Winfield Scott, the Commanding General of the United States Army, which contained the information of his projected campaign against Mexico City via Vera Cruz, and of the intended transfer of a large part of General Taylor's army to the new army then being assembled preliminary to being transported overseas by the Navy to Vera Cruz. General Scott's order, which closely followed his letter, directed the transfer from General Taylor's army of all the regular troops except four batteries of artillery and two companies of cavalry, as well as the veteran volunteer divisions of Generals Worth, Quitman, Twiggs, and Patterson.

General Scott advised General Taylor to fall back to Monterey and establish his headquarters there, but the old warrior could not brook the thought of a retreat, and decided to concentrate his depleted forces near Saltillo and to give battle, if necessary, at Buena Vista, a few miles south of that place.

General Santa Anna, who had become the military dictator of Mexico, had learned of the American plan of campaign by means of a captured dispatch, and decided to march north from San Luis de Potosi to Saltillo, a distance of about two hundred fifty miles for the purpose of defeating and destroying General Taylor's depleted and isolated army and then to return south in time to confront General Scott at Vera Cruz. It was a daring conception, which only needed success to make it Napoleonic.

Santa Anna began the march with some twenty-one thousand men including a large detachment of cavalry, but his army had dwindled to approximately sixteen thousand men by the time it reached the vicinity of Buena Vista, owing to the large losses suffered through desertion and sickness during its trying march across the desert country. The force which General Taylor was able to concentrate at Buena Vista amounted to approximately forty-five hundred men, including two troops of cavalry and four batteries of artillery, of which less than a quarter had, previously, been under fire. His only available reinforcements were three or four hundred men stationed at Saltillo to protect his supply base there from attack by a large Mexican cavalry force which threatened not only to capture his supplies but to cut his only line of retreat to the north as well.

On February 22, Santa Anna's strong advance cavalry arrived in front of Buena Vista, and found its further progress barred by General Wool's Division. Santa Anna decided to await the arrival of his infantry before attacking, and contented himself, in the meantime, with a demand for the surrender of the American Army, which was declined in forceful language.

The American position was a strong one. It lay across the San Luis de Potosi–Saltillo highway and the adjacent creek which paralleled it. The creek flowed through a deep maze-like gorge from which an amazing number of ravines ran in a southeasterly direction, to a mountainous area. The ravines and the plateaus lying between them lent themselves well to the defense. West of the creek the ground rose steeply until it became a line of high hills.

During the day, the American Army occupied the defensive position which had been previously selected. In the late afternoon, Santa Anna began the battle by a turning movement with the intent of enveloping and rolling up the American left flank.

The Mexican detachment succeeded by nightfall in gaining possession of the mountain which dominated the American left, but fighting ceased when darkness fell. The opposing armies bivouacked in the positions they then held, while General Taylor returned to Saltillo with the Mississippi regiment to supervise the construction of the defensive works there.

Early the next morning, Santa Anna renewed his attack. His major effort was directed against the American left, but he also launched powerful secondary attacks against the center. The tide of battle rose and fell and throughout the entire day the small American Army was again and again in imminent danger of destruction. In the forenoon, General Taylor with Colonel Jefferson Davis' veteran Mississippi Regiment arrived just in time to save the day on the left, as a newly organized Regiment had broken under an attack by superior numbers and had left the field with the exception of a small number of men who rallied around their gallant Colonel. At a later hour, the batteries of Captains Sherman and Bragg checked a powerful force making an attack on the center, in response to General Taylor's quiet words, "a little more grape, Captain Bragg." Everywhere on that historic field the decision trembled in the balance, as dauntless courage was displayed by American and Mexican alike. Finally, however, General Taylor enforced his unconquerable will on the enemy. He was truly the "Rock of Buena Vista," and the enemy waves of attack were broken as they repeatedly dashed themselves against that rock.

At nightfall, the fighting ended with the Americans still in possession of the stubbornly contested field. The night, though, was almost as hard as the day. In killed and wounded, General Taylor had lost six hundred seventy-three officers and men, among them Colonels Harden, McKee, and Clay, and many others of the bravest and the best. His troops were exhausted, and there was much confusion, owing to the mingling of units, the losses suffered, and the large number of stragglers who had left the field. A number of officers counseled a retreat under the cover of darkness. The old General, though, possessed the spirit of the true warrior. Calm, unhurried, and serene, he directed his commanders to reorganize their units, to round up their stragglers, to improve their positions, and to be prepared to renew the battle at dawn.

Santa Anna, too, faced a difficult and trying situation. His troops were discouraged by their unavailing attacks, and their morale was shattered by their heavy casualties. They were short of food and water. They had no near-by base from which supplies could be drawn. He had many powerful enemies in his rear who were plotting against him, and he knew that General Scott's campaign would soon begin. He lacked the indomitable spirit of his great adversary, the spirit which rose to its greatest heights in the face of danger or adversity. He, therefore, made the decision to retire from the field, and to march back to San Luis de Potosi in order to prepare to meet General Scott. The road on which he made that march was a veritable "Via dolorosa." He arrived at his destination with but the broken remnants of the proud army with which he had commenced the campaign. His prestige had been dealt a blow from which it never recovered.

His ability to resist the advance of General Scott's army was materially lessened.

Buena Vista played a part of far-reaching importance in the success of General Scott's campaign. It hastened the termination of the war. It added immeasurably to the glory of American arms. It made secure General Taylor's fame as a soldier. It, also, practically brought to a close his military career, as after two or three months spent, inactively, in garrisoning the towns and cities of northern Mexico, he was, upon his own request, relieved from duty there and then rejoined his family in their Louisiana home.

General Taylor was a splendid type of the old-time officer of the Regular Army. Although he lacked the advantages of West Point education and training, he was fitted by nature to be a soldier, and realizing his lack of military education, he devoted his energies to acquiring the requisite knowledge by study and in the hard school of experience.

He was affectionately known to his men as "old Rough and Ready." He was rough in appearance, scarcely ever wearing his uniform in campaign, and lived as simply and as roughly as did any of his soldiers, but he was always ready when the time for battle came.

Honor of the highest and strictest kind was his; straightforwardness was his unvarying rule. He never by any chance was guilty of subterfuge, and he scorned to do or say anything which savored in the slightest degree of chicanery or deceit. He told the unvarnished truth to his superiors no matter how disagreeable it might be, and to his subordinates he was equally candid. His rough exterior clothed the kindest and most unselfish of hearts and he was knit by hooks of steel to the hearts of his men.

It is not surprising, therefore, that this grand old soldier should have fired the popular imagination at home. After

La Resaca de la Palma, men began to say that he was of presidential timber. At first the voices were few, but, as time went by, the clamor increased. It was, however, disregarded by him, his invariable answer being that he had a duty to perform for his army and for his country, and could not, therefore, allow thoughts of political preferment to cloud his mind. He wrote to his friends that although a Whig, he was not a politician, and had always kept himself free of political activity throughout his career.

The transfer of his veteran troops to another army aroused the sympathy of the people. Then came suspense, and even the fear lest his little army of untried men should be destroyed. Suddenly rejoicing was universal among the people. His name was acclaimed and shouted from the house tops when the news of Buena Vista was spread abroad. His virtues were extolled at every fireside and his fame grew apace. He did not raise a hand to advance his own interests except, eventually, to write that he would accept the nomination if tendered him, and if elected, that he would do his best to serve his country well as President.

Finally the Whig convention met, and he was chosen from a field of candidates which contained such names as Daniel Webster, Henry Clay, and Winfield Scott. In the campaign which ensued, his Democratic opponent was Mr. Cass of Michigan, a man of much ability and of solid attainments. Taylor won with comparative ease.

"Old Rough and Ready" became President and fell heir to the sharp criticism which seems to be the inevitable lot of every man who has filled the exalted office of the Presidency. He kept his head in spite of it, however, and gave his country the full benefit of his common sense, his rugged integrity, and his exalted patriotism. He made a good

President, and the people knew it and loved him for his homely virtues, his modesty, his simplicity, and his courage.

His labors, however, were nearing their end. His tenure of office was brief. It continued for only sixteen months. On July 4, 1850, after attending a patriotic celebration in Washington, he was stricken by a severe illness, and a few days later, he died. His mortal remains were laid to rest in Louisville, Kentucky, near his boyhood home, while the whole nation grieved.

As Commander-in-Chief of the Army, Navy, and Marine Corps, President Fillmore published a general order from which the following extract is quoted : "The President of the United States with profound sorrow, announces to the Army and Navy and Marine Corps the death of Zachary Taylor, late President of the United States. He died at the Executive Mansion on the night of July 9, at half past ten o'clock. His last public appearance was while participating in the ceremonies of our national anniversary at the base of the monument now rearing to the memory of Washington. His last official act was to affix his signature to the convention recently concluded between the United States and Great Britain. The vigor of a constitution strong by nature and confirmed by active and temperate habits had in later years become impaired by the arduous toils and exposures of his military life. Solely engrossed in maintaining the honor and advancing the glory of his country, in a career of forty years in the Army of the United States, he rendered himself signal and illustrious. An unbroken current of success and victory, terminated by an achievement unsurpassed in our annals, left nothing to be accomplished for his military fame. His conduct and courage gave him this career of unexampled fortune, and with the crowning virtues of moderation and humanity, under all circumstances, and especially in the moment of victory, revealed to his countrymen those great and good qualities which induced them, unsolicited, to call him from his high military command to the highest civil office of honor and trust in the republic; not that he desired to be first, but that he was deemed to be worthiest.

"The simplicity of his character, the singleness of his purpose, the elevation and patriotism of his principles, his moral courage, his justice, magnanimity and benevolence, his wisdom, moderation, and power of command, while they have endeared him to the heart of the nation, add to the deep sense of the national calamity in the loss of a Chief Magistrate whom death itself could not appall in the consciousness of 'having done his duty.'"

The Governor of Virginia's order was issued over the signature of the Adjutant General and was as follows:

"The Commander-in-Chief having received intelligence of the death of Zachary Taylor, late President of the United States, and deeming it proper to mark by suitable demonstrations the general grief at a calamity so affecting to the Nation and to give expression to the reverence of a whole people for the memory of the illustrious dead:

"It is ordered that on tomorrow (July 15), the State House bell be tolled during the day and that the flag of the United States be displayed upon the capitol and at the Armory at half staff.

"That the principal entrances to the Capitol be hung with black.

"The Superintendent of the Virginia Military Institute will, on receipt hereof, cause suitable honors to be paid at that post to the memory of the late President

By Command

(signed) Wm. H. Richardson

Adjutant General."

The Superintendent's order follows :

"Headquarters,
Virginia Military Institute
July 29, 1850.

General Order No. 51.

"It becomes the painful duty of the Superintendent to communicate to the Corps of Cadets the accompanying official document of the death of Zachary Taylor, late President of the United States.

" With the general grief that pervades the whole American people, there is associated peculiar sadness when it is remembered that the Corps of Cadets was the last military body reviewed by the illustrious soldier and patriot.

"In obedience to the orders of the Governor there will be a suspension of duties and half hour guns will be fired from sunrise to sunset tomorrow.

"The officers and Cadets will also wear the usual badge of mourning for the period of thirty days.

By order of Colonel Smith"

Zachary Taylor ! You fought a good fight ! You did your duty fearlessly and well ! You kept the faith ! You have the admiration and the affection of the American people !

WOODROW WILSON

President of the United States

1913–1921

The Honorable JOHN BARTON PAYNE, The Speaker

FROM THE INTRODUCTION OF THE SPEAKER
by
GOVERNOR POLLARD

To revel in the things of the past simply for the sake of reveling is a useless pastime, but reviewing history for guidance and inspiration is both worthy and profitable.

Today we review the life of the last of the eight Presidents born in Virginia. A memorial to each, in pure white marble, has now been placed under the dome of our ancient Capitol whose rotunda has thereby been transformed into The Hall of The Presidents.

[209]

AT THE UNVEILING OF THE WILSON BUST

Showing Mrs. Wilson, Messrs. Pollard, W. C. Wilson, Daniels, Palmer, Glass, Payne, Redfield

When Washington appeared on the stage of history, American freedom was the issue.   When Wilson appeared, the freedom of the whole world was involved.

Washington led in the struggle for the liberties of his own country.   Wilson led in the struggle for the freedom of all nations.

Washington's sword established the league of states.   Wilson's pen inaugurated the League of Nations.

Washington's ideals were crowned with victory.   So it shall be with the ideals of Wilson.

HARRIET W. FRISHMUTH, *The Sculptor*

When the great war-President was confronted with the serious problems following the close of hostilities, he called into his official family, as his Secretary of the Interior, Hon. John Barton Payne. Judge Payne has served this country in many capacities, but in none has his service to mankind been more brightly reflected as in his present position as Chairman of the American Red Cross.

Though he reached distinction in another State, he has never forgotten Virginia, the place of his nativity.   He has given as a token of his affection for the Mother Commonwealth that wonderful collection of paintings which now adorns the walls of our Battle Abbey.

Virginia is grateful to him and welcomes him back home today to deliver the eulogy on the greatest Virginian of this generation.

This occasion is made more notable by the presence here today of Mrs. Woodrow Wilson and so many members of President Wilson's Cabinet and his close personal friend and physician, Admiral Cary T. Grayson.

I now present Mr. and Mrs. Louis Pennington, the generous donors of this bust.

I now present Miss Harriet W. Frishmuth, the talented sculptor.

WOODROW WILSON

ADDRESS BY

THE HONORABLE JOHN BARTON PAYNE

PERMIT me first to pay my tribute of appreciation to Governor Pollard for having so honored Virginia in wisely conceiving and splendidly carrying out his plan to honor her presidential sons by placing their busts in this historic Capitol. It was, indeed, a happy inspiration!

It has been only a little while since President Wilson was among us in the possession of his great powers and yet even now the world is filled with books and articles — some of them unkind — purporting to tell us with complete confidence and ample knowledge what manner of man he was. But for the name of the subject of such writings one could scarcely tell of whom they were written.

It was doubtless because of this that Governor Pollard desired to have some one who had worked with him and knew something of him in daily life to place on record in this historic setting knowledge and impressions of him gained by such contact and experience.

The life of Woodrow Wilson from his youth up was an open book. Born in Staunton, Virginia, December 28, 1856; his parents were Joseph Ruggles Wilson and Jessie Woodrow Wilson. The father was a Presbyterian clergyman of character, reputation, and ability.

In 1858 the father was called to a charge in Augusta, Georgia, and for a time was the teacher of the son. When he was fourteen the father was called to Columbia, South Carolina, as professor in the Columbia Theological Seminary. Here Woodrow entered a private school, later Davidson College, and in 1875, Princeton University. Meantime the family moved to Wilmington, North Carolina.

After graduating from Princeton in 1879, he entered the University of Virginia as a student of the law, remaining there through 1879-80, studying under John B. Minor. Ill health caused him to leave without graduating; his studies were continued privately. In 1882 he applied for, and obtained, admission to the Georgia Bar, passing with credit after an examination conducted in open court. Shortly thereafter he, in partnership with E. L. Renick, opened an office for the practice of law in Atlanta under the firm name of Renick and Wilson. For about a year, while waiting for clients, he occupied his time writing his first great work — *Congressional Government*.

The educational field seemed more attractive, and in 1883 he entered Johns Hopkins for a post-graduate course. Here he studied, taught, and wrote. For him 1885 was an important year. He finished — and Houghton Mifflin & Company published — his *Congressional Government*, which continues to be the leading American authority on the subject. This, and his work at Johns Hopkins, brought him an offer from Bryn Mawr of Associate Professor in History with an annual salary of $1,500. After Bryn Mawr, he became Professor at Wesleyan University, and in 1890 Professor at Princeton University.

Mr. Wilson's individuality was early manifest. Prizes for scholarship held no attraction for him. His mind was occupied with more serious things. To the curriculum he gave the attention necessary to pass his examinations with credit. The things which occupied his serious thought were his own writing and books on government, history, economics, and biography. The conviction early came to him that his usefulness would lie along these lines. That he would play his part in public life — probably in the Senate of the United States — is clearly foreshadowed in his studies and writings.

Gamaliel Bradford, who knew Mr. Wilson throughout his life, in his *The Quick and The Dead* speaking of this period of his life says : "Looking back from a later time, he said of his boyhood : 'I was born a politician and must be at the task for which, by means of my historical writing, I have all these years been in training.' Even when it seemed that circumstances had cut him off from a political career, he looked to it with bitter regret : 'I do feel a very real regret that I have been shut out from my heart's *first* — primary — ambition and purpose, which was to take an active, if possible a leading, part in public life.'"

In 1902 he became President of Princeton, serving eight years. For several years his work as President of Princeton met with universal praise and resulted in building up and greatly strengthening the institution. Later he endeavored to liberalize the University. This involved him in controversy, as to which I will quote Dr. Alderman, the great President of the University of Virginia, long intimately acquainted with Mr. Wilson and his work. In his masterful memorial of President Wilson, delivered to the Congress in the House of Representatives, he said : "The total effect on him of all this academic warfare was the hardening of his resolution, the acquisition of formidable political skill to gain his ends, the arousing of his passion for democracy, and the fixing of his purpose to rescue universities from material control. He was born to fight for the goodness which is at the heart of things, and this ideal quickly grew into an objective of freedom which caught

the eye of the Nation at the precise moment when a great
tide of liberal hope and opinion was flowing in and over a
generation of self-satisfaction and contentment with things
as they are.''

The fight he made at Princeton attracted such attention
in his State that he became Governor of New Jersey, and
two years later President of the United States, inaugurated
March 4, 1913.

Hard work had told upon Mr. Wilson. When he came
to the Presidency his health was poor; many supposed
he could not live through his term. I recall with what
solicitude one of his stanch Princeton friends, Mr. David
B. Jones of Chicago, told me of his precarious health and
of the fear that the President would not be able to stand
the strain of his great office. The responsibility, instead
of breaking him down, proved to be a tonic; his health
and strength improved and were equal to the demands
upon him.

While without experience in politics, he was well
grounded in the principles of our government. His
studies and writings were especially directed along these
lines and his knowledge of our institutions probably
greater than that of any former President.

It did not take him long to satisfy the country that a
great President had come to the White House.

Thoroughly typical of the man was his first inaugural
address — simple, straightforward, and so genuine that
it touched the hearts of the people; they realized that the
new President was indeed their friend and the friend of
mankind. I quote a brief extract : `` The Nation has been
deeply stirred ; stirred by a solemn passion, stirred by the
knowledge of wrong, of ideals lost, of government too often
debauched and made an instrument of evil. The feelings
with which we face this new age of right and opportunity

sweep across our heartstrings like some air out of God's own presence, where justice and mercy are reconciled and the judge and the brother are one. We know our task to be no mere task of politics, but a task which shall search us through and through, whether we be able to understand our time and the need of our people, whether we be indeed their spokesman and interpreter, whether we have the pure heart to comprehend and the rectified will to choose our high course of action. This is not a day of triumph; it is a day of dedication. I summon all honest men, all patriotic, all forward-looking men, to my side. God helping me, I will not fail them, if they will but counsel and sustain me!"

He never failed them!

The measures of his administration were stated so admirably by Dr. Alderman in his memorial address that you will, I am sure, thank me if I again quote him. He said: "Woodrow Wilson once said that the true teacher or the true artist or historian must always work for the whole impression. Working in this spirit, I cannot, at this time and place, attempt even to enumerate the legislative measures which, under his leadership, went forward in the Sixty-third Congress; but I venture to claim that no such well-thought-out program of financial, social, and industrial reform, no such inspiring spectacle of governmental efficiency and concentrated energy, no such display of fearless devotion to public interests, moving high above the plane of partisan advantage or of private gain, has been spread before the eyes of this generation as is afforded by the list of enduring enactments which crowned the accession to power of Woodrow Wilson."

One at least of these great measures should, in this period of economic stress, be emphasized. It has proved a bulwark of strength — I refer to the Federal Reserve Banking

Act. Without this our situation at this time would indeed be serious.

May I here quote an analysis of Mr. Wilson by Gamaliel Bradford? He says: "And first it is necessary to establish squarely the lofty ideal aims of Wilson's political life. To any one who has followed him at all closely the slurs of Roosevelt, 'he is astute and conscienceless, his lack of all convictions and willingness to follow every opinion,' are merely ridiculous. Wilson's aims may often have been unrealizable, but, if so, it was because of their loftiness. He wanted to govern, but it was because he saw the superb possibilities of government and fully appreciated the lamentable defects which had hitherto kept those possibilities unattained. He was not mad enough to say that he could remedy the defects, but he was man enough to say that he would give his brain and his whole soul and his very life to trying. Men had claimed too much for democracy. They had dallied with democracy and professed to have put it to the proof and found it a failure and they were beginning to laugh at it and throw it aside. He believed that democracy, for all its failures and defects, held the future of the world; as Lincoln believed it. He believed that democracy, rightly guided and interpreted, even perhaps through the dazzling conception of a world unity, held the only possible hope of the future, and he was ready to give all that was in him in every way to the attempt to realize that hope.

" Nor was Wilson by any means a mere dreaming idealist. He had fixed and definite and largely elaborated theories as to how the ideal should become a reality. Even as a boy he was an organizer, and all through his career he was inclined to make systematic plans and frame constitutions of one kind or another."

In 1914 the World War came. It was not long until

many well-meaning citizens at home and abroad began to insist that we should enter the War on the side of the Allies. When in May, 1915, the *Lusitania* was sunk and American lives lost, the demand became insistent. The President knew the time for us to enter the War had not come; he was not willing to involve the United States in war until it was manifest that the interests of our own country were clearly placed in jeopardy. He was waging a diplomatic controversy with Germany strongly protesting her submarine warfare. For a time it seemed possible he had won his fight; the submarine warfare grew less and seemed likely to cease. This hope was short-lived. Germany decided upon a ruthless campaign, doubtless believing that the submarines would harm the Allies more than the United States — should she join them — could do them good; reasoning that we had an insignificant army and could not raise and equip one of effective strength and transport it to the western front before — with the aid of her submarines — she could defeat the Allies.

The experience of the United States in the War of 1812, of 1861, and again in 1898, may have influenced her decision. Certain it is she concluded to ignore us. To her very great sorrow — she did not know President Wilson or the United States when fully aroused under his matchless leadership. The people speedily caught his inspiration and the glory of fighting a defensive war to preserve our institutions and to make the world safe for democracy, to destroy the power of the Kaiser, and to give men freedom in their lives, in their government, and freedom from future wars. War was declared, the United States standing with the President almost to a man.

What followed the declaration of war is an epic unparalleled in history. We had only a small army; we created one of four million men. We had no munitions; almost every factory in the United States was put to work. We had no ships; these we found or created. And so in every line of endeavor, with the result that Germany in an incredibly short time was confronted by the soldiers of the United States on the western front.

Almost of equal danger to their cause, the Central Powers encountered Woodrow Wilson speaking from the White House in Washington to their soldiers in their dug-outs, by their camp fires, and to the noncombatants at the family fireside — the language of peace, the language of hope.

Count Czarnin, Austrian statesman, said, "In the eyes of millions of people his program opened up a world of hope."

A French writer said, "It has been toward Wilson that our leaders have most turned. We looked to him as one might look at a clock."

The armies of the Central Powers began to melt; desertions were frequent. This and the vigorous attacks of the Allied and American armies caused all to realize that the end was near. On the eleventh of November, 1918, the end came and the allied world proclaimed Woodrow Wilson the hero of the peace by making his Fourteen Points the cornerstone of the Armistice.

Wilson had made his fight; the War was won. To him the world looked for the making of a peace which would satisfy the living that the dead had not died in vain.

The World War was unique in this: Our Chief Executive did not interfere with the command of the troops. President Wilson appointed General Pershing to the chief command; the President and the Secretary of War stood by him to the end; the public clamor for the appointment of distinguished men to command divisions in France made no impression upon him.

So with the organization of the civil population to supplement the departments of the Government in providing for the needs of the War. This mammoth task was done promptly, efficiently, and without scandal. When the administration changed in 1921, there was talk by political opponents of graft and scandal in the conduct of the war; lawyers and others were employed to investigate, but all to no avail — no graft — no scandal.

Why was this record possible? The President called for service men of the greatest worth in every walk of life; men whom he trusted; men whom the country trusted; men called for their merits, not their politics. The like had never before happened in the United States.

We come now to the Peace Conference.

Was Mr. Wilson wise in participating in the Conference?

So admirable a man as Claude G. Bowers in *Current History*, April, 1931, says: "It would have been better perhaps had he opened the Congress in Paris and then returned home." And "It would have been better had he placed some outstanding Republican leader, such as Taft or Root, upon the American delegation."

Like expressions are often heard. Is it possible that constant assertion may cause us to assent to a proposition we have not thought through? I can account for Mr. Bowers' statement in no other way.

Both propositions in my view are unsound; the first, that President Wilson should have opened the Congress and returned home — leaving the making of the peace to others — would have been like running away; utterly unlike Mr. Wilson and under all the circumstances down-right cowardly. The second — the appointment of Root or Taft — on its face appears plausible; the thought being that Senate opposition would have been lessened or removed. It must not be forgotten that before the Treaty reached the Senate it had to be negotiated. President

Wilson had thought through the peace settlement and had definite and clear convictions, not merely his own — but of the great mass of the people of the United States and the forward-looking people of the world, as to what should be accomplished for the peace and well-being of mankind. His Fourteen Points, embodying these principles, had been accepted by the Allies and formed the basis of the Armistice. It was essential that these should likewise form the basis of the Treaty. What he conceived the United States had been fighting for and must realize by the Treaty, simply stated, was: to make the world safe for Democracy; that is, self-determination for subject peoples and a Covenant of the Nations to make future wars impossible. For these principles he was prepared to fight to the end.

Is it probable that Mr. Root or Mr. Taft would have agreed with Mr. Wilson as to the supreme importance of these principles and been willing to follow him and work with him to place these Wilson principles in the Treaty of Peace? Is it not more probable that such strong men would have had their own views, which they would have preferred, or, if they accepted his principles, they may have disagreed as to the terms to be employed in the expression of the principle of self-determination or of the powers to be given the League of Nations. The differences which arose on the power to be enjoyed by the League of Nations occupy — as all know — many pages of the Congressional Record. If disagreement appeared even the probable result of such an appointment, it should not have been made.

Mr. Wilson was also convinced that unless the terms of the Covenant were made sufficiently strong to be effective, agreed upon early, and made an integral part of the Treaty, the Covenant would be sidetracked and in the end defeated or rendered colorless.

In the face of much opposition he succeeded at the plenary

session of January 25, 1919, in having the Covenant of the League of Nations made an essential part of the Treaty. Soon after this he sailed for the United States, appointing a member of his delegation to represent him in his absence. When he returned a month later, he found that two members of his delegation — one his representative — had consented to a procedure which in effect nullified the action of the plenary session as to the League of Nations. This greatly embarrassed the President and caused him to issue a statement to the press of such courage and sureness that there remained no doubt as to the leader of the Conference.

This is the statement:

"Paris, March 15, 1919.

"The President said today that the decision made at the Peace Conference at its plenary session, January 25, 1919, to the effect that the establishment of a League of Nations should be made an integral part of the Treaty of Peace, is of final force, and that there is no basis whatever for the reports that a change in this decision was contemplated.

"The Resolution on The League of Nations, adopted January 25, 1919, at the plenary session of the Peace Conference, was as follows:

"1. It is essential to the maintenance of the world settlement, which the associated nations are now met to establish, that a League of Nations be created to promote international coöperation, to insure the fulfillment of accepted international obligations, and to provide safeguards against war.

"2. This League should be treated as an integral part of the general Treaty of Peace, and should be open to every civilized nation which can be relied upon to promote its objects.

" 3. The Members of the League should periodically meet in international conference, and should have a permanent organization and secretariat to carry on the business of the League in the intervals between the conferences."

Chiefly by this bold move he was able to undo the mischief and to reinstate the League definitely in the treaty.

These facts are cited to suggest the difficulties which he encountered, even with his own friends, and the probability that greater difficulties — possibly insurmountable — would have arisen had political opponents been his associates.

Messrs. Root and Taft both prepared reservations. Mr. Taft sent a number to Mr. Wilson in Paris. Some were accepted and embodied in the Covenant; others not. Mr. Root prepared reservations which were presented to the Senate. Some of them, we know, were regarded by Mr. Wilson as harmful to the Covenant. This is not a criticism of these distinguished gentlemen, but an illustration of the manifest dangers which would have been likely to result in the defeat of the League of Nations and of the principle of self-determination had Mr. Root or Mr. Taft been appointed. If this seemed to Mr. Wilson probable, it shows how wise he was in assuming the responsibility for the negotiations and thus secure permanently in the treaty the principles for which we fought, the principles of the greatest and most lasting benefit to mankind.

While perhaps all persons may not agree with me, it is my conviction from a somewhat close observation at the time that, regardless of the personnel of the delegation, the Senate would not have accepted the Covenant of the League of Nations, unless reservations destroying its effectiveness were adopted.

In Mr. Wilson's mind there never was a doubt as to his duty to attend and take a leading part in the Peace Conference; nor as to what he would fight for. That clear and strong sense of duty arose from his own conviction as to what was essential. What this was no one else so fully understood or could so adequately and forcefully speak for the United States. This clearly appears from his address to the Congress of the United States delivered December 2, 1918, just before sailing for Paris. He said: "The peace settlements which are now to be agreed upon are of transcendent importance, both to us and to the rest of the world, and I know of no business or interest which should take precedence of them. The gallant men of our armed forces on land and sea have conspicuously fought for the ideals which they knew to be the ideals of their country. I have sought to express those ideals; they have accepted my statements of them as the substance of their own thought and purpose, as the associated governments have accepted them; I owe it to them to see to it, so far as in me lies, that no false or mistaken interpretation is put upon them, and no possible effort omitted to realize them. It is now my duty to play my full part in making good what they offered their life's blood to obtain. I can think of no call to service which would transcend this."

If undue modesty had caused him to remain at home and leave the making of the peace to others, it would, indeed, have been a tragedy.

Was the President's preparation for the work of the Conference adequate?

President Wilson could not have so touched the heart of mankind as to the possibilities of the peace without having given to the question profound consideration. His knowledge of the subject appears in all his utterances.

His speeches, made even during the war, show that he was thinking of the peace. At Mount Vernon July 4, 1918, he said, "These great objects (of the peace) can be put in a single sentence — What we seek is the reign of law based upon the consent of the governed and sustained by the organized opinion of mankind."

Apart from his own study of the subject, months before sailing for Paris some hundreds of distinguished scholars under the direction of Colonel House were at work in Washington preparing the essential data for use at the Conference.

Ray Stannard Baker, head of the Press Service at Paris and author of *Woodrow Wilson and World Settlement*, states : "Three days before the *George Washington* sailed into Brest Harbor, a blaze of glory, the President called together a group of the delegation for a conference. . . . The great body of the delegation was made up of geographers, historians, economists, and others upon whom the President was to depend for the basic facts to be used in the coming discussions. Many of these men had been at work for months in gathering material of every sort which might contribute to the solution of the problems raised at Paris. They had brought along with them in great boxes, now stored in the hull of the ship, a substantial library of books, documents, reports, together with a complete equipment of maps."

To these trained scholars he looked for the facts of history, of geography, racial lines, ancient and modern boundaries, international law, treaties, conventions; indeed, every essential, including all pertinent facts as to each state, colony, or other enemy possession. This did not always satisfy him. In dealing with some enemy countries he caused the appointment of commissions to go upon the ground and examine facts at first hand and to consult the inhabitants. In one case the other members of the big four declined to name their commissioners. He named two distinguished Americans who visited the country, made the necessary inquiry, and made their report.

Because mankind had accorded him the leadership in the making of the peace, he was appealed to by subject peoples within enemy territory and by persons suffering wrongs existing for generations.

To an American he said: "Yet you know and I know that these ancient wrongs, these present unhappinesses, are not to be remedied in a day, or with a wave of the hand. What I seem to see — with all my heart I hope that I am wrong — is a tragedy of disappointment."

To those who knew him knowledge of his thorough preparation and sympathetic attitude will cause no surprise.

A fact of the greatest importance which could not be anticipated was that before we entered the War the Allies had made secret treaties providing for the disposition and annexation of enemy territory. These treaties constituted the basis of the claims of the Allies for the spoils of war and were in conflict with the Fourteen Points and the Armistice resting thereon. They caused many and serious difficulties and sometimes acrimonious discussions.

Soon after the meeting of the Conference claims were presented by one or more of the Allied powers seeking the annexation of enemy territory based upon these treaties. Since all of the Allies were beneficiaries under one or other of the treaties, and the United States asked nothing for itself, Mr. Wilson found himself alone in opposition to the recognition of the treaties and strongly insisted that the subject peoples were no longer chattels to be passed from country to country, but human beings entitled to the right of self-determination; that the Treaty of Peace must rest upon facts and justice, and not upon secret bargains —

however well intentioned. The beneficiaries, on the other hand, insisted upon the integrity of the treaties and demanded the division of territory as agreed.

The contention of Mr. Wilson was denounced as new and revolutionary. In reply he pointed out that self-determination was a fundamental doctrine of the United States and was contained in the Declaration of Independence, the Virginia Bill of Rights, and the Constitution of the United States, all based upon the principle that governments rest upon the consent of the governed, and stated that as applied to war settlements his contention might appear to be new, but that war did not change the fundamental rights of mankind, and his contention was in keeping with the spirit of the age and of the purposes for which the United States entered the war.

The demands of the Allies were strongly pressed.

The British Dominions had been given by the treaties certain of Germany's African colonies. Mr. Lloyd George insisted that the Conference approve the treaties and award them the colonies in question and introduced into the Conference the Prime Ministers of the Dominions, who separately supported the claim. It was a crucial situation. Mr. Wilson urged that the colonies be given to the League of Nations to be governed by its mandatories.

Mr. Wilson's contention finally prevailed.

The Turkish countries presented a like question. The French, for instance, demanded Syria; Great Britain demanded Palestine. Mr. Wilson made the same contention as before, with the same result. France now governs Syria; Great Britain, Palestine; both as mandatories under the League of Nations.

March 11, 1917, France and Russia agreed upon the control of Poland and the dismemberment of Germany. Now Poland is a free and independent state and has recently erected a monument to the memory of Mr. Wilson. Germany, with small exceptions, remains intact.

Next consider the League of Nations. President Wilson not only insisted upon the creation of a League of Nations to prevent future wars, but that it should be brought immediately into being as an essential part of the Treaty and become a living force with certain definite powers, and an organization and a secretariat.

There was definite opposition to this program. Many were willing to create a League of Nations, but few were willing to give it effective power. If created as Mr. Wilson demanded, it might aid in the defeat of the claims arising under the secret treaties; Mr. Wilson contending that where peoples were not sufficiently civilized for self-determination the countries should be given to the League, and governed by it through mandatories. The contest, as you have observed, was long and bitter. Success finally crowned his efforts.

And yet Mr. Wilson's critics claim that he failed.

It is true the United States Senate, acting within its constitutional right, rejected the Treaty of which the Covenant of the League of Nations was, and is, an essential part; that in his great appeal to the people of the United States in support of the League Covenant Mr. Wilson was stricken and fell, holding aloft the banner of the Covenant in the sight of all mankind.

Was this failure? Did it wipe out or destroy the Covenant of the League of Nations? Did it destroy his masterful conduct of the War? Did it destroy his work at the Peace Conference? Did it take liberty and independence from Poland? Did it drive the subject peoples back into bondage?

No — nothing of his work was lost — the Covenant of the Nations, his heritage to mankind, remains a living force; Poland is free; the subject peoples retain the rights secured for them; other enemy territory remains under the League of Nations, governed by its mandatories.

The United States alone had failed!

Wilson, the soldier, fell on the field of battle!

Stonewall Jackson fell mortally wounded on the field of Chancellorsville, but the battle was won before Jackson fell. So the battle for mankind was won before Wilson fell.

What was this battle?

It was for the creation of the Covenant of the League of Nations that mankind might be forever saved from the horrors of war, that subject peoples might enjoy the right to live under a government which rests upon the consent of the governed.

This was the work of Woodrow Wilson; for this he died!

Was this failure?

A member of the delegation, steadfast and true, General Tasker H. Bliss, said : " The spirit created by the operation of the League brought about the Treaty of Locarno, the Briand-Kellogg Treaty, the Pact of Paris, renouncing war as an instrument of national policy. If the present League were to be dissolved tomorrow, the force of world opinion would recreate it stronger than ever and the first nation to demand its recreation would be the United States. It was Mr. Wilson who, by means of the Covenant, gave the world an opportunity to formulate an opinion. Out of his Covenant came a World Court of International Justice, which the world will never surrender. Like the League, if the Court be destroyed tomorrow, the world would find a great void that it knows would have to be refilled. A League and a Covenant in some form, both the offspring of Mr. Wilson's heart and brain, will be the eternal standard by which the world will judge the practicability of his idealism and in them will be found the full achievement of his task."

Of what other human being can so much be said?

There has been another like failure.

Almost a hundred and fifty years ago another great Virginian was accused of failure, and worse. Now all know him as, "First in war, first in peace, and first in the hearts of his countrymen."

And yet, on the day following his retirement from the Presidency in 1797, the leading paper of a great party spoke of him as follows: " ' Lord, now lettest thou thy servant depart in peace, for mine eyes have seen thy salvation,' was the pious ejaculation of a man who beheld a flood of happiness rushing in upon mankind. If ever there was a time that would license the reiteration of the exclamation, that time is now arrived, for the man (Washington) who is the source of all the misfortunes of our country is this day reduced to a level with his fellow-citizens, and is no longer possessed of power to multiply evils upon the United States. If ever there was a period for rejoicing this is the moment — every heart, in unison with the freedom and happiness of the people, ought to beat high with exultation, that the name of Washington from this day ceases to give a currency to political iniquity, and to legalize corruption. . . . When a retrospect is taken of the Washingtonian administration for eight years, it is a subject of the greatest astonishment that a single individual should have cankered the principles of republicanism in an enlightened people, just emerged from the gulph of despotism, and should have carried his designs against the public liberty so far as to have put in jeopardy its very existence. Such, however, are the facts, and with these staring us in the face, this day ought to be a jubilee in the United States." And even his own loved Virginia, in

[231]

this place so near the Battlefield of Yorktown — the culmination of his heroic sacrifices — refused to pass a resolution commending his administration as wise and patriotic.

What is the reflection? That the work of a great man must abide the judgment of posterity?

The refusal of the United States to accept the Covenant of the League of Nations, in view of the partisan character of the opposition, is not an argument against the Covenant, nor evidence of failure on the part of its author. The League in its strength as conceived by Wilson is now the property of the world; no power may take it away. Its future, its lasting benefit to mankind, rests with forward-looking men and women in all countries and in all time.

They will not let it fail!

While we meet here to honor the memory of Woodrow Wilson we hear the echoes of threatened war in the Orient. Instantly the world turns to his work — the League of Nations, the only organization, present or past, created by man to prevent war. The Government of the United States was almost the first to send its representative to Geneva; to announce full coöperation and to declare that it would sustain and support the League's action.

This result in a single decade!

This we certainly know: that a brave and fearless man who loved mankind conceived for humanity hope, peace, and freedom; and fought that these principles might be realized and remain forever its heritage — free from oppression; free from war. While fighting for these principles he died. It is said he did not love, and yet "Greater love hath no man than this, that a man lay down his life for his friends."